Scope

ILLICIT DRUGS

PEOPLE USE

USERS ARE THERE? HOW DO DRUGS AFFECT

CHILDREN AND THE FAMILY? DRUG USE

AND CRIMINAL BEHAVIOUR? WHAT ARE

THE COSTS ASSOCIATED WITH

PROBLEM DRUG USE? THE ARGUMENTS FOR

AND AGAINST LEGALISING PROHIBITED

DRUGS? WHAT ARE THE UK'S ANTI-DRUG

STRATEGIES? WHERE TO GET HELP? DRUGS

Drugs

your questions answered

A STUDENT READER

DRUGS AND THE MEDIA DRUG MYTHS

WHAT IS DRUG TESTING? ILLICIT DRUGS

AND THEIR EFFECTS WHY PEOPLE USE

DRUGS HOW MANY DRUG USERS ARE

THERE? HOW DO DRUGS AFFECT

CHILDREN AND THE FAMILY? DRUG USE

AND CRIMINAL BEHAVIOUR? WHAT

THE COSTS ASSOCIATED WITH

PROBLEM DRUG USE? THE ARGUMENTS FOR

AND AGAINST LEGALISING PROHIBITED

DrugScope is one of the UK's leading centres of expertise on drugs. Our aim is to inform policy development and reduce drug-related risk.

We would like to acknowledge the following for reprint permission: Headline, for Chapter 2, and Routledge and the Home Office for Chapters 5a and 5b respectively. We would also like to thank Mike Hough of the Criminal Policy Research Unit at South Bank University, Ross Coomber of the School of Social Science at the University of Greenwich, Trevor Bennett of the University of Cambridge, and Geoff Monoghan at the Metropolitan Police for their contributions and kind help.

Published by
DrugScope
32-36 Loman Street
London SE1 0EE
Telephone: 020 7928 1211
Fax: 020 7928 1771
E-mail: services@drugscope.org.uk
http://www.drugscope.org.uk

First published 1995
This second revised edition 2000

Edited by Gary Hayes
Editorial project management by Paula McDiarmid
Designed and typeset by Roger Harmar/Andrew Haig & Associates
Printed by The College Hill Press

Contents

illicit drugs and their effects

1

TEXT | **GARY HAYES** & **HARRY SHAPIRO**

YOUR | QUESTIONS | **ANSWERED**

What do various drug terms mean? | What

are the UK drug laws? | What risks are associated with drug taking? | What drugs

do people use and how? | What are their effects, prevalence, price, and legal

status, and where do they come from?

1 Introduction

The use of drugs for non-medical purposes is a complex aspect of human behaviour. Drug effects are strongly influenced by the amount taken, the surroundings, and the reactions of other people, as well as the mental and physical state of the user. These influences themselves relate to social and cultural attitudes to and beliefs about drugs, as well as more general social conditions. It is, therefore, generally misleading to make simple cause-and-effect statements, such as 'drug X always causes condition Y'.

This chapter deals only with illicit 'street' drugs and solvents, which, although not illicit as such, are certainly disapproved of when they are used for recreational purposes. This article does not deal with drugs like alcohol, tobacco or tranquillisers, although clearly there are major health implications associated with their heavy use. However, a minority of street-drug users also inject tranquillisers such as temazepam and diazepam.

The information in this chapter is only a summary. For more information on these or other drugs not covered in this article, please contact the DrugScope information service or refer to *Drug Abuse Briefing 7th edition*, DrugScope, 1999, available from DrugScope.

Drug terms

Addiction implies that a drug dependency has developed to such an extent that it has serious detrimental effects on the user. For example, s/he may be chronically intoxicated, have great difficulty stopping the drug use and be determined to obtain the drug by almost any means. The term has very negative connotations, inextricably linked to society's view of the drug user, and so medical experts now generally avoid it.

Dependence describes a compulsion to continue taking a drug in order to feel good or to avoid feeling bad. When this is done to avoid the physical discomfort of withdrawal, we speak of *physical dependence. Psychological dependence* describes the use of drugs as an emotional crutch that stimulates, gives pleasure or provides an escape from reality. It is recognised as the most widespread and most important of the two types of dependence.

Drug abuse and **drug misuse** are difficult to define, but essentially indicate a sense that taking a drug is harmful (abuse) or that its use is socially unacceptable (misuse). *Authorised medical use* of drugs is acceptable and not harmful, and therefore both terms overlap with the less subjective phrase, *non-medical use.* People who take drugs usually refer to themselves as 'using' drugs or as 'users'.

Problematic drug use refers to drug use resulting in social, psychological, physical or legal problems associated with dependence, intoxication or regular excessive consumption. In other words, it is not necessarily the frequency of drug use which is the primary 'problem', but the effects that drug-taking has on the user's life.

Street drugs refers to drugs which are sold illicitly. These can include drugs diverted from legitimate sources, such as Valium.

Tolerance refers to the way the body gets used to the repeated presence of a drug. It means that higher doses are needed to maintain the same effect.

Withdrawal effects are the body's reaction to the sudden absence of a drug to which it has adapted. The effects can be overcome by taking more of the drug, or by 'cold turkey' – ie, rapid withdrawal lasting up to a week.

Drug laws

There are two main UK laws relating to drugs. The Medicines Act 1968 governs the manufacture and supply of medicinal products of all kinds. The Misuse of Drugs Act 1971 aims to prevent the non-medical use of certain drugs.

Drugs controlled under the Misuse of Drugs Act 1971 (ie, "illegal drugs") are classed according to the penalties associated with offences involving that drug: offences involving Class A drugs attract the highest penalties, those involving Class C the lowest. It is an offence to possess any controlled drugs or to supply them to someone else without legal authority. Some drugs are only legally available on prescription.

It is also an offence to allow anyone on your premises to produce or to supply (give away or sell) illegal drugs, even if the person only offers to supply the drugs. It is also an offence if one or both parents know about, but do nothing to prevent, their son or daughter from sharing illegal drugs with a friend in their house. It is an offence to permit the smoking of cannabis or opium in your house. To supply or offer to supply any article, except syringes and needles, believing that it will be used to prepare controlled drugs or to administer them (to yourself or others) in an illegal context is also an offence.

Maximum penalties for offences against the Misuse of Drugs Act are severe. First offenders charged with the possession of drugs that are for their own use are likely to receive only a caution. However, others may be fined (which gives them a criminal record), and regular offenders, people selling drugs, or drug smugglers might well be imprisoned. The maximum penalty for drug trafficking (ie, supplying or selling) offences is life imprisonment.

Anyone who finds what they think is an illegal drug, must destroy it or hand it without delay to someone authorised to possess illegal drugs, usually a police officer.

Drug-taking and risk-taking

Most people who use drugs come to no harm, but there are some very serious dangers that apply to any type of drug.

1

1

Overdoing it

Taking too much at once risks an experience that gets out of control and causes distress or even fatal overdose. Obviously, the more that is taken, the higher the risk of harm.

A psychoactive drug (ie, a drug that affects the mind) taken in high doses over a long period is likely to distort a person's perception of, and response to, her/his environment. This could impair normal physical functioning and development.

As tolerance and dependence develop, greater quantities of drugs are needed, and the problems of financing drug purchases can lead to deterioration in diet and general lifestyle, and can threaten housing and employment stability.

Intoxication lessens inhibitions and health awareness. Unprotected sex runs the risk of an unwanted pregnancy and contracting diseases such as chlamydia, HIV and venereal disease, to name but a few.

Wrong time, wrong place

Even in moderate doses, most psychoactive drugs impair motor control, reaction time, and attention span. These effects can last several hours. No matter how people feel, they are not as capable as before. When driving, operating machinery or crossing roads, they are more dangerous to themselves and to others.

Many drugs amplify mood. So if someone is depressed, anxious or aggressive, drugs can make things a lot worse. Even drugs which are thought of as calming (like alcohol and tranquillisers) can release aggressive impulses because they weaken social and personal inhibitions.

Individual differences

Statements about drug effects often are either about what might happen in extreme cases, or about what usually happens with most people. But not everyone is 'most people'. For instance, some people develop a toxic reaction to a single cup of coffee. Individuals with psychotic tendencies may be pushed over the brink by their experiences under the influence of powerful hallucinogens like LSD. Drug effects also vary with body weight. In general, less heavy people are more affected than heavier people on the same dose.

Adulteration and mistaken identity

Drugs offered on the illicit market are often not what they are claimed to be. If illicitly manufactured, they are likely to contain impurities or adulterants. The buyer can never be sure how strong the substance is. This adds greatly to the unpredictability of the effects of drugs obtained either without medical supervision or the quality control which is imposed on licit manufacturers.

Getting caught

Most people get drugs from their friends and then pass them to other friends. Many are unaware that if caught by the police they can be treated as possessing and supplying a drug – otherwise known as dealing. Prosecution for any drugs offence can damage job and emigration prospects – causing indirect social or economic harm to those convicted. These are risks that most drugs users and dealers accept, and some possibly seek, as part of drug culture.

Doubling up

The dangers of any drug are likely to be increased if it is taken while another drug is still in the body (ie, 'doubling-up'). Doubling-up on depressant drugs (alcohol, solvents, opiates, tranquillisers) is probably the most dangerous. Complex interactions can occur between other types of drugs, and loading one drug on top of another multiplies the risk.

Pregnancy

There are two major ways in which drugs might damage a foetus. Firstly, heavy use may affect the mother's health, either directly or indirectly through self-neglect and poor nutrition. Secondly, drugs may reach the foetus through the mother's bloodstream, and its immature bodily processes are less able to cope than those of an adult. These risks are by no means the same for all drugs, and little is known about these effects.

In general, heavy drug use in pregnancy is associated –(probably for a variety of reasons) with premature birth and low birth weight. There is also an increased risk of the baby dying around the time of birth. On the other hand, research on the effects of moderate drug use is generally inconclusive and many heavy drug users give birth to perfectly healthy babies. But this is an under-researched area, and doctors generally advise pregnant women not to take drugs if it can be avoided (see page 66, What are the effects of drugs on the foetus).

Injection

Injection is the least-used method of taking drugs but also the most hazardous. When injected, the drug enters the bloodstream immediately and some of it is carried directly to the brain, producing an effect within seconds. For this reason, all the effects of the drug are more intense, the user is incapacitated more quickly, and the risks become more serious.

HIV and hepatitis can be introduced through sharing blood-contaminated, non-sterile syringes or needles. People who are HIV positive may develop AIDS, or they may not have any symptoms and may not develop AIDS for several years or possibly not at all. From the moment they are infected, however, they carry the virus in their blood, and can infect other people through sexual intercourse sharing injecting equipment.

Other major dangers of injecting are overdose, abscesses, septicaemia, gangrene and damage from using crushed tablets and other dosage forms not meant to be injected. When a drug is injected dependence is more likely for three reasons: high doses are common, drug users enjoy the rush, and the injection ritual may become as important to the user as the effects of the drug itself. Nevertheless, dependence is not inevitable and takes time to develop.

1

1 The drugs

AMYL AND BUTYL NITRITE
Poppers

Amyl, butyl and isobutyl nitrite (known collectively as alkyl nitrites), are chemically related to nitrous oxide (laughing gas) and are inhaled. They are clear, yellow, volatile and inflammable liquids with a sweet smell when fresh, but when stale degenerate to a smell often likened to dirty socks.

What does the law say?
Amyl nitrite is classified in the UK as a pharmacy medicine under the Medicines Act 1968, but butyl nitrite is not. This means amyl nitrite is theoretically available from any chemist without a prescription. However, recent concerns about its use have caused the Medicines Control Agency (MCA), which administers the Medicines Act, to restricted it to a prescription only medicine. The MCA has stated, in effect, that it can decide which substances count as medicines and thus fall under the Medicines Act. This position is also underpinned by a European directive that allows, without any change in UK law, poppers to be classed as medicines regardless of how they are sold. This has yet to be tested out in court. The prosecution of a retailer in a case brought by the Royal Pharmaceutical Society in 1996 was settled out of court and so cannot be counted as legal precedent.

Who makes it and who buys it?
Butyl nitrites available for non-medical use are largely produced in the USA and marketed in the UK by wholesalers to the sex and dance industries. In terms of the effects of the substances, there appears to be little to choose between any of the brands or between any of the nitrites.

They are easily available in sex shops, joke shops, so-called 'head' shops (retailers of drug paraphernalia), at dance events, or by mail order. They are sold under such trade names as Rush, Locker Room, Ram, Rock Hard, TNT, Liquid Gold, Thrust, and Hardware. Poppers usually retail in Britain for around £5 per 10ml bottle, although prices may vary from region to region, depending on who is selling the drug and when. The price in a London gay club might be £10 a bottle while at a music event in Glasgow the same product might be only £3.

Generally, poppers have been associated with the gay community. A survey in 1994 by Project LSD found that 70 per cent of gay men, or men socialising in the same environment, have used the drug.[1] However, recent surveys suggest that the drug is becoming more common among the wider population including younger teenagers. It is estimated that 13 per cent of those aged between 16 and 29 years have used the drug.[2]

Poppers

What are the short-term effects?

Once inhaled, the effects are virtually instantaneous and last for 2-5 minutes. There is a 'rush' as the blood vessels dilate, the heartbeat quickens and blood rushes to the brain. As a result, pounding headache, dizziness, a flushed face and neck and light-headedness are commonly reported. Those using the drug to enhance sexual pleasure claim a slowed sense of time, prolonged sensation of orgasm and prevention of premature ejaculation, although some have reported problems with achieving erection. Alkyl nitrites relax the body's soft muscle tissue – eg, the muscles surrounding the eye and the anal sphincter.

Less common physical symptoms include nausea, weakness and cold sweats. A painful burning sensation results from spilling nitrites on the skin.

Blood pressure is reduced, which could cause unconsciousness, especially if the user is lying down to inhale and then gets up quickly. Excessive use may result in a reduction of oxygen in the blood known as methaemoglobinaemia. Symptoms can include cyanosis, when the skin and lips become blue-tinged, severe vomiting, shock and unconsciousness. An acute attack of this condition has caused fatalities, but usually in those who have swallowed rather than inhaled nitrites.

What are the long-term effects?

Tolerance develops within two or three weeks of continual use, but after a few days of abstinence, this tolerance is lost, leaving the user particularly vulnerable to headaches if use is resumed. There are no reports of withdrawal symptoms or psychological dependence – although repeated use as a sex aid and stimulant is not uncommon.

Because the drug is excreted rapidly from the body, there appear to be no serious long-term consequences from the inhalation of nitrites by healthy adults. Cases of nitrite dermatitis have been reported, affecting the upper lip, nose and cheeks, sometimes accompanied by pain and swelling of the nasal passages resembling sinusitis. This clears spontaneously in about 10 days and only reoccurs with resumed use.

The use of alkyl nitrites has been linked to the development of a rare cancer known as Kaposi's sarcoma, which is one of the earliest symptoms of AIDS in gay men who are HIV positive. The link was made because most of the earliest AIDS

1

1

cases were gay men who had used nitrites, which possibly contain carcinogenic compounds, but there were conflicting studies on this. Currently there is even less support for the theory, although it may still be the case that, along with many other substances, nitrites act to depress the immune system. However, the significance of this in the development of AIDS is not known, and many study results are inconclusive.

AMPHETAMINES
Speed, uppers, whizz, Billy, Dexedrine, dexies, Ritalin

Amphetamines are stimulants in the form of synthetic powders available as a variety of tablets, capsules, etc – sometimes in combination with other drugs. These have a medical use and in the 1950s and 1960s they were widely prescribed for depression or to suppress appetite. They are now only recommended for the treatment of pathological sleepiness and (paradoxically) hyperactivity in children. Amphetamines may be swallowed in tablet form, or sniffed, smoked, or injected as a powder.

Amphetamine powders

What does the law say?
Amphetamines and similar stimulants are 'prescription-only drugs under the Medicines Act 1968. With the exception of some of the milder forms, they are also controlled under the Misuse of Drugs Act as a Class B drug, but as Class A if prepared for injection. Doctors can supply them and patients can possess them when they have been prescribed. Apart from this their production, supply and possession are offences. Allowing premises to be used for their production or supply is also an offence.

Who makes it and who buys it?
After cannabis, amphetamine is the most-used illicit drug in the UK, with one in ten adults having used the drug.[3] Street amphetamine is usually amphetamine sulphate powder illicitly manufactured in the UK or Northern Europe.

Illicit amphetamine is heavily cut (often between 5 and 15 per cent purity) and sells for around £10-£15 a gram. An occasional user might consume ½ gram in a few weeks . A heavy user who has developed substantial tolerance might consume several grams a day of relatively impure amphetamine.

What are the short-term effects?
Amphetamines arouse and activate the user in much the same way as the body's natural adrenaline does. Breathing and heart rate speed up, the pupils widen, and appetite lessens. The user feels more energetic, confident and cheerful. Because of

these effects, there is a risk of psychological dependence.

As the body's energy stores become depleted, the predominant feelings may become anxiety, irritability and restlessness. High doses – especially if frequently repeated over several days - can produce delirium, panic, hallucinations and feelings of persecution.

The effects of a single dose last about three to four hours and leave the user feeling tired, but often unable to sleep due to the residual stimulant effect of the drug. It can take a couple of days for the body to fully recover.

What are the long-term effects?
To maintain the desired effects, the regular user has to take increasing doses, often many times the normal dose. When they eventually stop, they are likely to feel depressed, lethargic and ravenously hungry. Amphetamines merely postpone fatigue and hunger and do not satisfy the need for rest and nourishment. Heavy use risks damaged blood vessels or heart failure, especially for people with high blood pressure or pulse rates and those who take strenuous exercise (eg, athletes) while using the drug.

Regular high-dosage users are liable to develop delusions, hallucinations and paranoia. Sometimes these develop into a psychotic state, from which it can take several months to fully recover. Heavy use also debilitates the user due to lack of sleep and food and lowers resistance to disease, all of which can have serious effects on health.

CANNABIS
Hash, spliff, blow, draw, toke, grass, weed, marijuana, skunk
Cannabis derives from *Cannabis sativa* (although other strains exist), a bushy plant easily cultivated in Britain. It is generally used as a relaxant and a mild intox-

Pipes typically used to smoke cannabis

1

1

icant. The most important active ingredients, tetrahydrocannabinol (THC) and cannabinoids, are concentrated in the resin at the top of the plant. Hashish or hash is resin scraped from the plant and compressed into blocks. It is the most commonly-used form in the UK. Herbal cannabis (grass) is a weaker preparation of the dried plant material. Increasingly however, stronger 'designer' forms of herbal cannabis are being grown in this country from seeds imported from Europe (eg, skunk, northern lights). Less common in the UK and strongest of all, is cannabis oil, a liquid usually prepared from the resin.

In the UK, cannabis is prepared into joints or spliffs and smoked, often in combination with tobacco. Cannabis can also be smoked in a pipe, brewed as a drink, or used in cooking.

What does the law say?

Cannabis is strictly controlled under the Misuse of Drugs Act, and is a class B drug. It is illegal to cultivate, produce, supply or possess, unless a Home Office licence has been issued for research or other special purposes. It is also an offence to allow premises to be used for cultivating, producing, supplying or smoking cannabis.

Who makes it and who buys it?

Cannabis is the most widely-used of all the drugs controlled under the Misuse of Drugs Act. It is now established in the leisure activity of large sections of the population – latest surveys suggest that perhaps eight million people have tried the drug, with 1.6 million using it every month.[4]

At street level, imported herbal cannabis retails for about £70-£120 an ounce, resin for £25-£35 a quarter ounce. Skunk, on the other hand, tends to be much more expensive at £120-£200 an ounce. Eaten, £1.50's worth of resin would be sufficient to produce the desired effects. Smoked, about the same or slightly less could be used to make a couple of cannabis cigarettes sufficient for two or three people to get mildly intoxicated. Recreational users might consume an eighth of an ounce a week; heavy and regular cannabis users, that amount in a day.

What are the short-term effects?

The effects of cannabis depend largely on the expectations, motivations, and mood of the user, the amount used and the situation. Most people do not experience very much at first and have to learn which effects to look out for.

The most common, and most sought-after, effects are talkativeness, bouts of hilarity, relaxation and greater appreciation of sound and colour. While intoxicated, the cannabis smoker will be less able to perform tasks requiring concentration or intellectual or manual dexterity. Some of these effects can be reduced with sufficient application and concentration however.

There may be perceptual distortion with higher doses. People who use the drug when anxious or depressed, may find that their unpleasant feelings are magnified, and can sometimes experience short-term panic. The same is true of inexperienced people using high doses. There is virtually no danger of fatal overdose.

The effects generally start a few minutes after smoking, and may last up to one hour with low doses and for several hours with high doses. There is no hangover of the type associated with alcohol, although some may feel tired, light headed and possibly edgy the next day.

What are the long-term effects?
There is no conclusive evidence that long-term cannabis use causes lasting damage to physical or mental health in the vast majority of users,. However, as with tobacco, cannabis smoke probably causes bronchitis and other respiratory disorders if frequently inhaled, and may cause lung cancer. Cannabis may therefore cause special risks for people with lung, respiratory or heart disorders. Heavy use in people with disturbed personalities can precipitate a temporary psychiatric disorder.

Cannabis does not seem to produce physical dependence. Regular users can, however, come to feel a psychological need for the drug or may rely on it as a social lubricant. As with other sedating drugs, people chronically intoxicated on cannabis may appear apathetic, sluggish and neglect their appearance, but there is no evidence of a special cannabis amotivational syndrome, where users become chronically lethargic and unmotivated.

COCAINE AND CRACK
Coke, Charlie, snow, 'C', crack, rocks

Cocaine is a white powder derived from the leaves of the Andean coca shrub, with powerful stimulant properties similar to those of amphetamine. It is commonly sniffed or snorted up the nose through a tube and absorbed into the blood supply via the nasal membranes. It is also injected and smoked, the smokable variety being known as crack.

What does the law say? Cocaine, its various salts, and the leaves of the coca plant, are controlled under Class A of the Misuse of Drugs Act. Cocaine can be prescribed, but otherwise it is illegal to produce, possess or supply it. It is also illegal to allow premises to be used for producing or supplying the drug.

Who makes it and who buys it? Cocaine and crack use appear to be on the increase in the UK. The recent British Crime Survey estimates that 3 per cent of the adult population have used cocaine. As with other drugs, cocaine and crack use is greatest among younger adults, with 6 per cent of 16 to 24 year olds reporting having used it.[5] The powder costs around £40-£100 for a gram of 50 per cent pure drug. Although sold in small rocks (about raisin size) at about £20 per rock, crack costs about the same per gram, but can be up to 100 per cent pure compared to cocaine which is usually 40 to 50 per cent pure. The intermittent user might sniff ¼ to ½ gram of powder over two or three days. Regular crack users with sufficient supplies might consume several grams a day.

1

Cocaine is usually snorted using a rolled banknote

What are the short-term effects?

Like amphetamine, cocaine produces physiological arousal accompanied by exhil-aration, decreased hunger, indifference to pain and fatigue, and feelings of physical strength and mental capacity. Sometimes these desired effects are replaced by anxiety or panic. When sniffed, the psychological effects peak after about 15 to 30 minutes and then diminish. This means the dose may have to be repeated every 20 minutes to maintain the effect. When smoked, the effects are felt more immediately and wear off more quickly.

Large doses, or a spree of quickly repeated doses, can lead to an extreme state of agitation, anxiety, paranoia and, perhaps, hallucination. These effects generally fade as the drug is eliminated from the body. The after-effects of cocaine include fatigue and depression, though in comparison to amphetamines and ecstasy, these effects are less profound. Excessive doses can cause death from respiratory or heart failure, but these are rare.

What are the long-term effects? There are no clear-cut tolerance effects with cocaine. Nor are there withdrawal effects of the kind that require the user to con-tinue taking the drug to avoid feeling ill. However, cocaine users may develop a strong psychological dependence on the feelings of physical and mental well-being it affords and are often tempted to step up the dose. After discontinuing, the user will feel fatigued, sleepy and depressed, all of which reinforce the temptation to repeat the dose.

With heavy and frequent use, increasingly unpleasant symptoms develop. Euphoria is replaced by an uncomfortable state of restlessness, hyper excitability, nausea, insomnia and weight loss. These generally persuade people to cut down or stop for a while. Continued use may lead to a state of mind similar to paranoid psychosis. Regular users may appear chronically nervous, excitable and paranoid. All these effects generally clear up once use is discontinued. Repeated sniffing can damage the membranes lining the nose and may also damage the structure separating the nostrils. Prolonged smoking may cause a number of respiratory problems.

ECSTASY
'E', pills, Mitsubishis, MDMA, doves, elephants

Ecstasy, or MDMA (methylenedioxyamphetamine), is classed as a hallucinogenic amphetamine, a group of drugs with effects roughly combining those of amphetamines and LSD. Although developed in 1912, ecstasy did not become widely used until the emergence of the 'acid house' scene in the late 1980s, and has been associated with dance music and parties ever since.

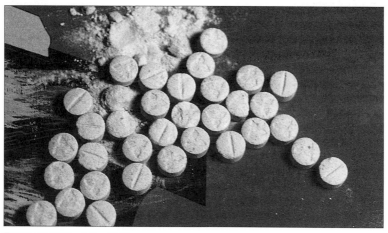

Ecstasy tablets – Mitsubishis

What does the law say?
Ecstasy is a Class A drug. No doctor can prescribe it and anyone wanting to use it for research purposes has to obtain a licence from the Home Office.

Who makes it and who buys it?
Since its association with the acid-house movement in the late 1980s and early 1990s, use of the drug has become common among ravers and others not necessarily connected with the music scene. Indications are, however, that with the demise of the acid house scene, and the increased use of other stimulants such as cocaine and amphetamines, ecstasy use may be falling among younger users, particularly in the south-east. Roughly one in ten 16-29-year-olds have used the drug, with roughly 2 per cent using regularly.

Ecstasy is sold in various types of capsules and tablets of differing shapes and

1

colours for anything between £8-£15 a tablet. As the drug has become more popular, so the quality has tended to decrease – many tablets and capsules sold as ecstasy may not contain any active drug at all, be a mixture of other drugs, or be (deliberately) below the active dosage (therefore encouraging the user to take another pill in order to 'come up' – ie, feel the effects of the drug).

What are the short-term effects?
MDMA is effective at the moderate single dose level of 75-100mg. Effects are experienced after 20-60 minutes and can last several hours. Pupils become dilated, the jaw tightens and there can be brief nausea, sweating, dry mouth and throat, a rise in blood pressure and pulse rates, and loss of appetite. There can be some difficulty with bodily co-ordination making it dangerous to drive or operate machinery. At doses above 200mg, or if the drug is being used repeatedly over a few days, all these effects may be experienced more acutely. Once the drug has worn off, there may be some residual effects similar to those experienced by amphetamine users, including fatigue and depression, which can last for several days.

As with LSD, whether the experience is bad or good often depends on the mood and expectations of the user. With moderate levels of use, most users report a mild euphoric rush followed by feelings of serenity and calmness, and the dissipation of anger and hostility. Most bad experiences with the drug have been reported by those using higher doses over a period of time. Effects include anxiety, panic, confusion, insomnia, psychosis, and visual and auditory hallucinations. These generally die down once the drug is stopped, but can leave the user in a weakened mental and physical condition for a while. Some of these effects have been experienced by those who have tried the drug for self-therapy and have then been unable to deal with the emotions that using MDMA has brought to the surface.

So far around 80 deaths directly associated with the effects of taking ecstasy have been recorded in otherwise apparently healthy young people. Most of these young people collapsed at raves or shortly afterwards and all exhibited symptoms associated with severe heatstroke. The current best guess is that these users have succumbed to the cumulative effects of taking MDMA while dancing for long periods in a very hot, humid atmosphere.

What are the long-term effects?
There is evidence from research carried out by the National Poisons Unit of an association between ecstasy use and liver damage. Tolerance to the effects of MDMA develops, but there is no physical dependence, no heroin-like withdrawal symptoms nor any evidence that MDMA is used compulsively for years.

Overall, the literature suggests that people should not take MDMA if they suffer from heart disease, high blood pressure, glaucoma, epilepsy or are in poor physical or mental condition. Women with a history of genito-urinary tract infection should not use the drug. There is no evidence that the drug has any effect on the foetus or causes problems in the newborn.

Increasing documentation is emerging on the effect of ecstasy on brain cells and brain function. A number of studies on animals (mainly rats, monkeys and squirrels) have shown that MDMA can cause permanent neurotoxic damage to serotonin-producing parts of the brain – serotonin, a neurotransmitter, is involved the enhancement of mood and memory. While animal studies may say little about human behaviour, some human studies suggest that MDMA is similarly neurotoxic in humans. One such study has shown that self-reporting ecstasy users had possible damage to serotonin producing areas (decreased serotonin transporter binding sites).[6] Although these results are significant, they must be interpreted with caution. Not only does the measure for ecstasy use rely on self-reporting, which may be incorrect or omit the use of other substances, there is also concern that the researchers failed to fully control for pre-existing serotonin function abnormalities, which could be a cause or caused by ecstasy use. Nor do we know the exact functional effects of the apparently damaged areas, and so can say little about what behavioural effect, if any, this will produce.

HEROIN AND OTHER OPIATES

'H', brown, skag, smack, junk, methadone, meth, Diconal, dikes, codeine

Opiates are drugs derived from the opium poppy. Opium is the dried milk of the poppy and contains morphine and codeine. From morphine it is not difficult to produce heroin, which is, in pure form, a white powder more than twice as potent as morphine. Opiates have medical uses as painkillers, cough suppressants and anti-diarrhoea treatments. A number of synthetic opiates are manufactured as painkillers. These include pethidine, dipipanone (Diconal), dextropropoxyphene (Distalgesic) and methadone (Physeptone), a drug often prescribed for opiate addiction.

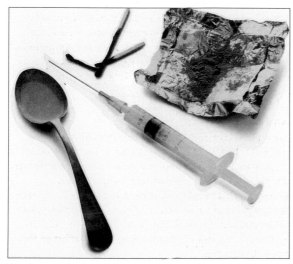

Heroin and injecting equipment

1

1

Opiate powders can be swallowed, or dissolved in water and injected. Heroin can be sniffed up the nose like cocaine, or smoked by heating it and inhaling the fumes; this is know as 'chasing the dragon'.

What does the law say?

Opiates are controlled under the Misuse of Drugs Act. This makes it illegal to supply or to possess them without a prescription, or to produce, import or export them without authority. It is also an offence to allow premises to be used for producing or supplying these drugs. Only specially licensed doctors can prescribe heroin or dipipanone for the treatment of opiate addiction. All other opiates can be prescribed for normal therapeutic uses. Heroin, morphine, opium, and methadone are Class A drugs.

Who makes it and who buys it?

Since the late 1970s there has been an apparently rapid rise in heroin use and heroin dependence, both injecting and smoking. Doctors, drug services, hospitals and many other agencies notify the Home Office of clients who come to them with problem drug use. During the six months ending September 1998 there were nearly 35,000 people in Britain reporting to services for their drug use, a majority of whom (57 per cent) were using heroin. But there are likely to be many thousands more who do not come forward for treatment.[7]

Increasing evidence suggests that use of this drug is on the increase among younger people and is common in certain areas, although not necessarily impoverished areas.[8] There is concern that younger users are unaware of the addictive potential of smokable brown and are buying it in smaller more affordable deals, therefore using it regularly and without caution.

Fifty per cent pure heroin sells for £80 to £100 a gram, although it is increasingly being sold in smaller £25 or £10 wraps containing a quarter or eighth of a gram. It is usually cut with a variety of powders of similar appearance, including glucose powder, caffeine, flour, talcum powder, and drug substances like phenobarbitone powder. A heavy user might use 1/4 gram a day.

What are the short-term effects?

Moderate doses of pure opiates produce a range of generally mild physical effects (although the painkilling effect will be marked even at moderate doses). They depress the nervous system, including reflex functions such as coughing, respiration and heart rate. They also dilate blood vessels (giving a feeling of warmth) and depress bowel activity, resulting in constipation.

Low doses produce euphoria. Higher doses produce sedation and the chance of overdose, where the user can go into a coma and possibly die from respiratory failure. Overdose is more likely if other depressant drugs, like alcohol, are used at the same time, and there can be fatal reactions to injected adulterants.

Opiates induce a relaxed detachment from pain, desires and anxiety. They make people feel drowsy, warm and content, and relieve stress and discomfort. However, among people who have developed physical dependence and tolerance, positive pleasure is replaced by the need to obtain opiates in order to stay normal.

Along with, or instead of, these reactions, first use (especially injection) often causes nausea and vomiting. These unpleasant reactions quickly disappear with repeated doses. The effect of sniffing heroin is slower and less intense than that of intravenous injecting. The effects of heroin are felt as quickly after smoking as after intravenous injecting, but are not so intense. Heroin can be addictive no matter how the drug is taken, including smoking, eating and sniffing.

What are the long-term effects?

As tolerance develops, regular users increase the dose to achieve repeated euphoria. Sudden withdrawal after several weeks on high doses, results in varying degrees of discomfort, comparable to flu. The effects start 8-24 hours after the last dose and include aches, tremor, sweating, chills, sneezing, yawning and muscular spasms. They generally fade in seven to ten days, but feelings of weakness and loss of well-being last for several months. People can overdose when they take their usual fix (the amount taken)after a break during which tolerance has faded.

Physical dependence is not as significant as the strong psychological dependence developed by some long-term users. Dependence of any kind is not inevitable and many people use heroin on an occasional basis without experiencing problems.

The physiological effects of long-term opiate use are rarely serious in themselves. But physical damage, associated largely with repeated, often unhygienic, injecting and with the injection of adulterants, is common among long-term users. Injectors also run the risk of HIV infection unless they always use sterile equipment. Repeated heroin sniffing can damage the membranes lining the nose. Decreased appetite and apathy can contribute to illness caused by poor nutrition and self-neglect. As tolerance and dependence develop, financial difficulties can also contribute to self-neglect and a diminished quality of life.

KETAMINE

Special K, 'K', Ketalar

Ketamine is an anaesthetic with analgesic and psychedelic properties chemically related to phencyclidine (PCP, or angel dust). Like PCP, ketamine is a dissociative anaesthetic – ie, patients feel detached and remote from their immediate environment.

What does the law say?

Ketamine is not controlled under the Misuse of Drugs Act and possession is not a criminal offence. It is however, a Prescription Only Medicine under the Medicines Act, meaning that unauthorised supply is illegal.

1

1

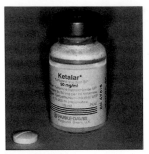

Ketamine tablets

Who makes it and who buys it?

It is not known whether illicit supplies have been illicitly manufactured from scratch or reformulated from licit sources such as hospitals or vets. However, it is possible that, currently, street ketamine derives from licit sources, where diverted liquid is heated to evaporate the water, leaving ketamine crystals. The drug is retailed like other illicit drugs such as ecstasy, often replacing that drug when not available. Prices range from £6–£25 for a wrap of powder.

Ketamine appears to be widely used on the dance scene. One small study estimated that nearly 25 per cent of those who took drugs at dances and clubs had tried ketamine.[9]

Ketamine comes in a variety of forms ranging from its liquid pharmaceutical state, for injecting, through to pills to be taken orally. Powders are sniffed up the nose or sometimes smoked.

What are the short-term effects?

Ketamine takes effect over varying time periods depending on the route of administration (from 30 seconds for intravenous injection to 20 minutes taken orally), and the effects can last up to three hours. The normal dose for sniffing ketamine is about 100-200mg. Used intravenously or intramuscularly, a sub-anaesthetic dose would be around 1-2mg per kg of body weight. Ketamine effects are dose-specific, with roughly 100mg sniffed resulting a stimulant effect, and 200mg and above causing more hallucinatory and out-of-body experiences.

Reported physical effects include an initial cocaine-like rush, vomiting and nausea, slurring of speech and vision, numbness and ataxia (irregular muscle coordination). Many users report a temporary paralysis and a feeling of being out of the body.

Aside from the risks from injecting common to all drugs, it is ketamine's anaesthetic properties which pose the main physical dangers. Under its influence, users are less likely to feel pain and, combined with the fact that some might not realise they are hallucinating (because they believe what is happening is real), there is the potential for serious injury.

As with any anaesthetic, eating or drinking in the hours prior to use could cause vomiting; because of the risks of choking, this could be particularly dangerous if too much is taken and the user falls unconscious. If the dose exceeds the standard surgical dose, then there is the risk of respiratory collapse or heart failure. However, ketamine deaths appear to be rare; only one case is cited anecdotally in the literature with no precise reference given.

Users report that although ketamine's psychological effects come on and recede faster than with LSD, these effects are similar – including hallucinations, synaesthesia ('seeing' sounds and 'hearing' colours), euphoria, de-personalisation and confusion, plus the powerful dissociative or out-of-body (flying or floating) sensations, which appear specific to ketamine. Different from the LSD experience, however, are the reported feelings of aggression and stimulation. A recent article in *DrugLink* highlights the addictive potential of ketamine, primarily because of the powerful detachment and heightened visual and potentially spiritual experiences which occur.[10]

With repeated use, tolerance develops quickly. One medical anecdote describes having to give a child 250 per cent more of the drug after just 12 treatments during surgery.[11] Evidence suggests that once a level of tolerance is developed, it is not reversible.[12]

What are the long-term effects?

The literature on the consequences of long-term ketamine use is sparse, and the following observations are invariably based on single case studies. Flashbacks, (short-lived recurrences of the drug experience) similar to that experienced by some LSD users are possible. One clinical report suggests there may be memory, attention and vision impairment from long-term use, which in this case did not return to normal once use was reduced.[13]

Physical dependence and withdrawal are not a feature of ketamine use, although as stated, the psychological power and detachment can make it an addictive drug for some users. Tolerance develops quickly. Stimulant-like weight loss and loss of appetite can occur during periods of heavy use.

One authority has concluded that frequent and prolonged use of ketamine could cause the same problems as PCP, including psychological dependence, psychosis and gradual loss of contact with the real world.[14]

KHAT

Catha edulis, commonly known as qat or qaadka in Somalia or chat in Ethiopia, but now referred to consistently in the literature as khat, is a green leafy plant chewed by people in northern Africa and Arab countries. Khat contains two known pharmacologically active substances, cathinone (aminopropiophenone) and cathine (norpseudoephedrine).

Cathinone is the main active ingredient. Its concentration in the fresh leaves ranges from 0.3 to 2.1 per cent depending on the origin and variety of the plant.

1

Cathine concentrations range from 0.7 to 2.7 per cent. The active ingredients start to deteriorate two days after the plant has been harvested, and therefore the leaves must be chewed when fresh.

Khat leaves

What does the law say?

The khat plant itself is not controlled under the Misuse of Drugs Act, but the active ingredients, cathinone and cathine, are Class C drugs. Cathinone may not be lawfully possessed or supplied except under a licence for research, though cathine may be prescribed.

Who makes it and who buys it?

The khat plant is cultivated throughout eastern Africa and the Arabian peninsula at altitudes of 1,500 – 2,000 metres. There are several varieties of the plant, but the two most commonly imported are: Miraa, chiefly from Kenya, and Harari from Ethiopia. Plants are imported into the UK either as fresh leaves or sometimes as twigs. The plant can be purchased at some specialist health food shops, markets and in a number of 'head' shops. Prices vary, but a small bundle of leaves weighing 2-3 ounces will cost roughly £4.

Somalis in Britain are the main group associated with khat in the British press. Khat is used also to some extent by people from Ethiopia and the Arabian peninsula. There is little evidence to suggest khat is being used in the UK except among these communities.

What are the short-term effects?

Khat is predominantly stimulant in effect. A typical khat chewing session is said to be the equivalent of ingesting a moderate 5mg dose of amphetamine sulphate. Following mild euphoria and talkativeness, users often report calming effects.

Because it is chewed, khat affects the oral cavity and the digestive tract. Inflammation of the mouth and other parts of the oral cavity, with secondary infections, are common in khat users.

What are the long-term effects?

There is evidence that excessive use of khat can lead to other health problems such as heart disease and loss of sex drive in men. Of particular concern is the risk of oral cancer, reportedly prevalent among khat chewers in Yemen. Prolonged and excessive use can bring on psychological problems such as depression, anxiety and irritation, sometimes leading to psychosis.

LEGAL HIGHS

Herbal ecstasy

Herbal ecstasy has, until recently, been sold freely at raves, clubs, concerts and festivals. It contains various herbs and extracts that are claimed to be hallucinogenic and/or stimulant. Packaging and vendors claim that it is a natural and safe substitute for ecstasy. However, they often have side effects similar to many synthetic drugs.

A hallucinagenic formula from USA

Ephedrine and Ma Huang

Ephedrine is an extract of the Chinese herb Ma Huang, which has been reported to have stimulant effects such as shivers up and down the spine, sensitive skin and muscles, and feelings of exhilaration. In China, Ma Huang is sold as a medicine and an aphrodisiac. In the UK, it is sold as Cloud 9, Nirvana Plus and other herbal highs said to mimic ecstasy.

Yohimbe

Yohimbe (also spelled yohimbine) is derived from the Yohimba tree roots and is said to be an aphrodisiac. It is sold as an hallucinogenic with stimulant effects, and marketed as Yohimbix[8] or an additive to other herbal highs.

Salvia

Salvia is derived from the American plant *salvia divinorum*, a member of the mint family. It is used in shamanic rituals by the Mazatecs and other groups in Meso America. Salvia is marketed in the UK as herbal ecstasy – eg, Eclipse. It is sold as a herbal remedy in health food shops and chemists under its botanical name. Its effects are more hallucinatory than the other legal highs and it has some stimulants properties.

What does the law say?

Herbal highs are not controlled under the Misuse of Drugs Act, and therefore possession is not an offence as long as it is for personal use. The Home Office has expressed concern at the free sale of these drugs, which has led recently to the Medicines Control Agency treating them as medicines. Unauthorised manufac-

1

ture and distribution, therefore, can be treated as an offence under the Medicines Act. However, this law does allow the drug to be legally imported for personal use only. As with poppers, enforcement is difficult, and many unauthorised outlets avoid prosecution. The position is made more confusing because related compounds such as pseudoephedrine, found in over-the-counter preparations such as Nurofen – and some decongestants, are categorised as General Sales List (as are Ma Huang and yohimbe when sold as a herb), which means they can be sold by any retail outlet.

Who makes it and who buys it?

Imported as a herb in its raw form, yohimbe is grown in Asia, ephedrine in China, Japan and North America. Ephedrine (and pseudo-ephedrine) is also produced by a number of pharmaceutical companies as an additive in cough and cold remedies such as nasal decongestants. Salvia is grown in North America and distributed from Holland and the USA. It is sold by specialist herbal shops, sex shops and head shops, at dance events and by mail order – the USA is a main source of imported herbal ecstasy pills. Prices vary but usually four to six tablets or capsules retail for roughly £15 to £20 .

As yet there are no statistics on the level of use in the UK.

What are the short-term effects?

Packaging often states that these drugs, because they are natural and herbal, are safe or non-addictive. Any drug that has a psychological effect can be difficult to stop taking if it is used regularly. Proper, controlled research on these drugs is sparse and therefore side effects and possible dangers when taken with other drugs, and even foods, is not fully known.

Within approximately 45 minutes of being eaten, yohimbe raises blood pressure and increases heart rate. The drug has alleged aphrodisiac properties, increasing sensuality and sexual desire. The hallucinations are said to be quite strong and the effects on the body similar to that of ecstasy.

Ephedrine has effects similar to ecstasy, although physical sensations are more pronounced. Side effects can include racing heart, dry throat, anxiety, tremor, and cold feet and hands.

Little research has been carried out on the short- and long-term effects of salvia. Users report stimulant properties similar to ephedrine, coupled with hallucinations at higher doses. It is often therefore likened to magic mushrooms. The main active ingredient is thought to be salvinorum.

Concern has been raised that ephedrine and yohimbe, particularly the latter, when taken with certain drugs and a number of amine-specific foods, can prove toxic. Cases have been reported of individuals collapsing after taking yohimbe with foods such as chocolate, cheese, sherry, pineapples, bananas and others containing tryptophans. Taking ephedrine and yohimbe in combination with MAOI drugs (anti-depressants) may also contribute to high blood pressure.

What are the long-term effects?

The long-term effects of yohimbe, salvia and ephedrine use are not well documented. Regular use can lead to problems associated with hypertension such as dizziness, glaucoma, and heart disease. As with most stimulants, repeated use can result in users feeling fatigued, possibly anxious and paranoid leading to psychotic episodes.

LSD

Acid, trips, tabs

Lysergic acid diethylamide (LSD) is a synthetic white powder. Minute amounts are generally mixed with other substances to make tablets or capsules, which are swallowed. The drug is normally absorbed onto brightly-patterned paper squares (tabs), and can be absorbed onto gelatine sheets or sugar cubes. The strength of these preparations varies.

A selection of LSD tabs

What does the law say?

LSD (and other hallucinogens) is strictly controlled (Class A) under the Misuse of Drugs Act. It is illegal to produce, supply or possess it except in accordance with a Home Office licence issued for research or other special purposes. It is also an offence to allow premises to be used for its production or supply.

Who makes it and who buys it?

LSD use (often called a 'trip') is quite common among young people in the drug scene. Just over one in ten 16-29-year-olds have taken LSD. Tabs containing LSD (one or two of which are sufficient for a trip) cost £2-£3 each.

What are the short-term effects?

A trip begins about half an hour after taking LSD, peaks after two to six hours, and fades out after about 12 hours, depending on the dose. It usually progresses through several phases. Experiences whilst on LSD are hard to describe. This is partly because they vary but also because they can be at variance with our accustomed view of the world. Effects depend very much on the user's mood, the setting, who they are with as well as the dose. Effects often include seeing intensified colours and experiencing visual or auditory distortions. It is difficult to combine a trip with a task requiring concentration, and driving will almost certainly be impaired.

1

Emotional reactions may include heightened self-awareness and mystical or ecstatic experiences. A feeling of being outside one's body is commonly reported. Physical effects are generally insignificant. Unpleasant reactions (bad trips) may include depression, dizziness, disorientation and sometimes panic. These are more likely if the user is unstable, anxious, or depressed, or in hostile or unsuitable surroundings.

Deaths due to suicide or hallucinations, though much publicised, are rare. Most deaths connected to LSD are accident-related or involve other drugs.

What are the long-term effects?

There is no reliable evidence of physical damage from repeated use of LSD. The main hazards are psychological rather than physical. Serious anxiety or brief psychotic reactions may occur, but can usually be dealt with by friendly reassurance. Prolonged, serious adverse psychological reactions are rare. They are most likely in individuals with existing psychological difficulties.

Brief but vivid re-experiences of part of a previous trip have been reported, especially after frequent use. These can leave the person feeling disorientated and can be distressing, but are only very rarely dangerous.

There is no physical dependence, and frequent use is discouraged by the fact that for several days after taking LSD further doses are less effective .

HALLUCINOGENIC MUSHROOMS

Several species of mushrooms can have hallucinogenic effects when eaten. About a dozen of these grow wild in the UK, notably the liberty cap. The liberty cap contains the hallucinogenic chemicals psilocybin and psilocin. It may be eaten fresh, cooked or brewed into a tea, and can be preserved by drying. Due to variations in potency, it is impossible to say how many mushrooms are required for a hallucinogenic experience; 20 to 30 is a general amount, but much fewer may suffice.

Distinguishing hallucinogenic from poisonous (and possibly deadly) mushrooms is a complex skill, requiring knowledge of botany and expertise in mushroom classification.

Magic mushrooms or liberty caps ready to eat

What does the law say?

It is not illegal to pick and eat magic mushrooms. However, they contain psilocin or psilocybin which are Class A drugs. If anything is done to the mushrooms such as boiling or crushing them or even drying them out, the person could be accused of making a 'preparation or other product' containing psilocin or psilocybin and so charged with possessing a Class A drug.

Who makes it and who buys it?

Roughly one in ten 16-29-year-olds have taken magic mushrooms. The liberty cap is the most commonly occurring and most commonly used species in the UK. It is also the most consistently potent. It appears between September and November. *Amanita muscaria* is also common in early autumn. However, its unpleasant side-effects, and the likelihood and dangers of mistaken identity, limit its use as a recreational drug. The fungi are usually picked and eaten soon after or passed onto friends. Some are sold on, usually fetching £5 for a pack of 100.

What are the short-term effects?

The effects of psilocybin- and psilocin-containing mushrooms are similar to a mild LSD experience. However, the effects come on more quickly and last for a shorter time. At low doses, euphoria and detachment predominate. At higher doses, visual distortions progress to vivid hallucinations. Commonly, there are feelings of nausea, vomiting and stomach pains. Bad trips can occur and may develop into a psychotic episode. These are most common after repeated or unusually high doses, or if the user is inexperienced, anxious or unhappy. They can usually be dealt with by friendly reassurance.

There have been reports of longer lasting disturbances, such as anxiety attacks and flashbacks to the original experience, but these almost invariably fade. By far the greatest danger is the possibility of picking a poisonous mushroom by mistake.

What are the long-term effects?

Like LSD, tolerance rapidly develops – eg, twice as many liberty caps may be needed on a subsequent day to repeat an experience of the day before. This discourages frequent use. There are no significant withdrawal symptoms or physical dependence. Individuals may, however, feel a desire to repeat their experiences. No serious effects of long-term hallucinogenic mushroom use have been reported, but no studies have been undertaken to assess the effects of extended frequent use.

SOLVENTS

Glue, butane, lighter fuels, aerosols, cleaning fluid

Some organic (carbon-based) substances produce effects similar to alcohol or anaesthetics when their vapours are inhaled. Several have applications as solvents (in glues, paints, nail varnish removers, dry cleaning fluids, de-greasing com-

1

1

pounds, etc). Others are used as propellant gases (in aerosols and fire extinguishers) or as fuels (eg, petrol, cigarette lighter gas). The effect of inhaling a solvent can be heightened by increasing the concentration of the vapour and/or excluding air – eg, by sniffing from inside a plastic bag placed over the head.

Solvents come in many forms and packages

What does the law say?

Under the Intoxicating Substances (Supply) Act 1985 it is an offence to supply or offer to supply solvents to persons aged under 18 if the supplier has reason to believe that they intend to misuse them. The Cigarette Lighter Refill (Safety) Regulations 1999, on the other hand, removes the onus of intention by making it an offence to sell butane refills to anyone under 18 years of age, regardless of whether the retailer is aware of its intended use. In Scotland, it is an offence to "recklessly" sell solvents to children knowing they intend to inhale them. Other than this, selling, possessing or sniffing solvents is not restricted. Sniffers may be convicted for unruly, offensive or intoxicated behaviour or because they resist police attempts to intervene. Someone driving under the influence of solvents may be convicted of driving while unfit.

Who makes it and who buys it?

Glues and most other sniffable products are easily available in shops. The government has published guidelines for retailers, advising them to stock these products out of reach of children and for staff to refuse to sell them to children whom they suspect may misuse them. Solvent misuse has always tended to be more popular among younger children, as they cannot afford to buy drugs or are too young to go into pubs. However, the recent fall in deaths from solvent misuse may mean that solvent misuse is becoming less fashionable as younger people have easier access to drugs. Prevalence varies from school to school and region to region. Roughly 3 per cent of 14-15-year-olds in England have tried solvents, with girls often outnumbering boys.[15]

What are the short-term effects?

Inhaled solvent vapours are absorbed through the lungs and rapidly reach the brain. Part of the effect is due to reduced oxygen intake. Body functions like breathing and heart rate are depressed. Repeated or deep inhalation can result in an 'overdose, causing disorientation, loss of control, and unconsciousness, from which, in normal circumstances, sniffers quickly recover. The experience is very like being drunk. Experienced sniffers may go on to seek dreamlike experiences. Generally, these are not true hallucinations as youngsters do not confuse them with reality.

The effects of solvent vapours come on quickly, and disappear within a few minutes to half an hour if sniffing is stopped. Afterwards the user may experience a mild hangover (headaches, poor concentration) for about a day. Sniffers run the risk of accidental death or injury if they are intoxicated in an unsafe environment, such as on a roof or by a canal bank. Sniffers can die from choking on vomit if they sniff to the point of unconsciousness. If the method used to inhale the solvent obstructs breathing (eg, large plastic bags placed over the head) and the sniffer becomes unconscious, death from suffocation may result.

Some products (notably aerosol gases and cleaning fluids) sensitise the heart and can cause heart failure, especially if sniffers exert themselves at the same time. Gases squirted' directly into the mouth can cause death from suffocation.

What are the long-term effects?

Very long term (eg, ten years), heavy solvent misuse might result in moderate, lasting impairment of brain function, affecting especially the control of movement. Chronic misuse of aerosols and cleaning fluids has caused lasting kidney and liver damage. Repeatedly sniffing leaded petrol may result in lead poisoning.

Despite these possibilities, lasting damage attributable to solvent misuse seems extremely rare. In Britain, surveys of groups of sniffers have not revealed any persistent medical consequences.

While someone is sniffing repeatedly, pallor, fatigue, forgetfulness and loss of concentration can become a recurring daily pattern. This could affect their performance and functioning and there can be weight loss, depression and tremor. These symptoms will tend to clear up once sniffing is discontinued.

Tolerance develops, but physical dependence is not a significant problem. Psychological dependence develops in a minority of susceptible youngsters with underlying family or personality problems. These people will probably become lone sniffers as opposed to the usual pattern of sniffing in groups.

1. Smith R (1995) 'A report on the findings of project LSD's: Preliminary survey into lesbians, gay men and bisexuals' drug use', London: Project LSD.

2. Ramsay M and Partridge S (1999) *Drug Misuse Declared in 1998: Results from the British Crime Survey*, London: Home Office.

1

1

3. Ibid.

4. Ibid.

5. Ibid.

6. McCann U D, Ridenour A, & Shaham Y (1998) 'Positron emission tomographic evidence of toxic effect of MDMA ("Ecstasy") on brain serotonin neurons in human beings', *Lancet*, 352, 1433-37.

7. Department of Health (1999) 'Statistical Bulletin: Statistics from the Regional Drug Misuse Databases for six months ending September', London: DoH.

8. Eggington R & Parker H (2000) *Hidden heroin users: Young people's unchallenged journeys to problematic drug use* Manchester: SPARC.

9. Release (1997) *Release Dance and Drugs Survey – An Insight into the Culture* London: Release.

10. Jansen K (2000) 'Anaesthetic addiction: Ketamine part 1: hits and myths' in *DrugLink*, 15 (1), p 8-11.

11. Byer D E & Gould A B (1981) 'Development of tolerance in ketamine in an infant undergoing repeated anaesthesia', *Anaesthesiology*, 54, p 255-6.

12. Jansen K (2000) 'Anaesthetic addiction: Ketamine part 2: addictive psychedelic', *DrugLink*, 15 (2), p 18-21.

13. Seigel R K (1978) 'Phencyclidine and ketamine intoxication: a study of recreational users', in Peterson R C & Stillman R C (eds) *Phencyclidine Abuse: An Appraisal*. Maryland: NIDA Research Monograph 21.

14. Ibid.

15. Balding J (1999) *Young People in 1998 – and looking as far back as 1983*, Exeter: Schools Health Education Unit.

why 2 people use drugs

TEXT | **MARTIN PLANT**

YOUR | QUESTIONS | **ANSWERED**

What physically is it that makes people use drugs? |

What is it in a person's personality that makes them use drugs?| What things

around us influence why we take drugs? | What historical reasons are

there for drug use in today's society? | Why do drugs feature so

strongly in our's and other's society?

from Plant M *Drugs in Perspective*, Hodder and Stoughton, 1987.

2

A daunting number of suggestions have been put forward to explain why people use drugs and why some users become dependent on them. Many of these theories are speculative and anecdotal, stemming from personal experiences and observation of a few drugtakers rather than from rigorous research. Most theories about the *causes* of drug use or drug dependence rely upon descriptions of *established* drugtakers. There is very little information about the characteristics of these individuals before they become involved in drugs. For this reason there has been frequent confusion between the *causes* of drug use and its apparent *correlates* or even *consequences*.

Most British studies of drug users have been confined to highly selective groups such as students or people in treatment institutions. The significant differences noted between different groups such as heroin dependants in a clinic or cannabis smokers in a college have been largely responsible for the different causal theories put forward. Virtually every writer on the subject of drug use has ventured some opinion, but most have highlighted themes that are relevant to *their* particular study group of drugtakers and which may have little relevance to others. While a perplexing number of equally plausible and useful theories co-exist, few people would suggest that either drug use in general or drug dependence are caused by any single factor. It seems that drug use in general is the outcome of interactions between the drug, the personal characteristics of the individual and their environment. It is clear then that drug use stems from many reasons and is the subject of many research interests. It is equally clear that it would be unrealistic to conclude that research in any single field has all the answers.

That said, three general types of theory have been suggested. These are constitutional, individual and environmental.

Constitutional (or biological) approaches

These are concerned with either biological predispositions or with the relationship between a drug and the body.

It has been suggested that depressant drugs such as alcohol, barbiturates and tranquillisers might appeal to those in need of relaxation while stimulants, such as cocaine and amphetamines, might appeal to extroverts who are predisposed to hyperactivity. Animal research has shown that sometimes there does exist a genetic predisposition to use specific drugs. There is a growing body of evidence that inherited factors can predispose some people to develop alcohol-related problems. Such factors obviously interact with availability, social context and other important influences on drug use.

In recent years considerable interest has been aroused by the discovery that the body produces opiate-like substances. It had been known for over 20 years that the human brain has specific receptors for opiates. It now appears that these receptors, in addition to responding to externally produced opiates such as morphine and heroin, respond to a group of internally produced *peptides*. Some of these substances, called endorphins (literally 'the body's own morphine') closely resemble opiates. The receptors excited by such substances are concentrated in the pathways of the brain that are concerned with the perception of pain. In consequence it is an important and intriguing possibility that the development of opiate dependence by some people, or even the general use of certain drugs, may be explained by the ability of some substances to modify the perception of profound experiences such as pleasure and pain.

Individual approaches

Individual approaches are largely concerned with either unusual personality traits (in the case of drug dependent individuals) or far more general factors such as extroversion which may explain willingness to experiment with cannabis or to indulge in other forms of drug use.

Personality characteristics

It is a commonplace belief that drug dependence is at least partly attributable to personality abnormalities, and many studies have supported this conclusion. Even so, the evidence for this view is confusing to say the least, because it is based upon a comparison of 'drugtakers' with 'others'. It does appear that opiate users are probably more neurotic than 'normal' people, but this is not a universal conclusion. And although some institutionalised drugtakers have been noted to exhibit higher than average 'hostility scores', they are not unique in so doing. There are, after all, plenty of neurotic, hostile non-drug users. More generally, it has been noted that if any kind of drug is widely acceptable, as is alcohol, then there is no reason at all why users should have unusual personalities.

Intelligence

Evidence shows that drugtakers are of average or above average intelligence. This conclusion is supported by studies of drugtakers in treatment, educational and penal institutions and in the general population. It is clear that drugtakers vary a great deal in many respects, and there is little support for the view that drug use in caused by lack of intelligence.

General psychiatric state

It is evident that drug dependants in treatment institutions are often psychiatrically disturbed. Sometimes this could result from drug misuse, but there is also evidence that sometimes individuals displayed signs of disturbance before becoming drugtakers. Case history data are often cited to support the view that drug taking satisfies a variety of psychological needs and that sometimes drug dependence is secondary to a clearly defined psychiatric illness. However, it is possible of course that both psychiatric disturbance and drug taking may be caused by some other factor. It cannot necessarily be assumed that they invariably lead to one another.

2

2

Gender

Men appear far more likely than women to use psychoactive drugs (tranquillisers and depressants excepted) and to be heavy users or dependent upon such substances. There may be many explanations for this. Biological or personality differences between the sexes may predispose men to be drugtakers. Certainly social pressures have traditionally inhibited women even from using legal and socially approved drugs (although these inhibitions are waning – there is evidence to suggest that young women are now more likely to smoke than young men).

Age

Most illegal drug users are young, as are most of those who experience alcohol-related problems. There has been much speculation about whether or not age affects drug dependence. It is probable that youthful anxieties and sexual uncertainties may encourage the use of certain drugs. Also the menopause in women, and old age in general, may often generate pressures that make drug use attractive. On the other hand, if drug use is attributable to personality predispositions, there is no reason why it should be especially prevalent among certain age groups.

Drug use as self-medication

Most drugs have clearly defined effects. It is possible that people who have high anxiety levels or other psychological needs use drugs specifically for this reason, to adjust their 'unsatisfactory' mental state to a more acceptable level. Many drug users certainly report that they use drugs 'to get high', 'to feel relaxed', 'for the experience'. People who are drug dependent also frequently account for their reliance upon drugs in similar terms – 'I use drugs to stop being depressed.'

It is difficult to assess how truthful or perceptive such accounts are. Precise motivation for complex acts are hard to pin down accurately. The main problem is that one cannot guess what would have happened if drugs had not been used. That depression and anxiety are commonplace among drug addicts is not reason enough to conclude that they adopted drug use as a calculated means of countering such conditions.

Hedonism

Drugs can be fun. They offer an accessible and often reliable means of obtaining enjoyable experiences. Anyone who doubts this should remember that most adults use drugs (alcohol, tobacco, coffee) and appear to accept uncritically that such use is valuable. By their own admission, drug users make it abundantly clear that they take drugs in the most part because they like it. By definition, drugs alter the user's mental state – slowing, speeding or distorting perceptions – and many autobiographical accounts of drug use emphasise the appeal of these effects.

A basic human need?

As noted above, psychoactive drug use is virtually universal in some form or other. It has been suggested that this may be so because there is a basic human need to experience an altered state of consciousness. This is compatible with the fact that most people use drugs and most people are clearly not psychologically disturbed. This is really a philosophical theory but it merits consideration in the face of the willingness of such huge numbers of people to use drugs in whatever way and for whatever effect.

Curiosity

Numerous studies of drug use in social settings report that curiosity is often stated to be the reason for initial drug use. This is as true of alcohol and tobacco as it is of cannabis, LSD, solvents, cocaine or opiates. This view, propounded by the drug-takers themselves, may however be partisan. Even if curiosity does account for initial drug use, it does not explain why some users become dependent while others do not.

Self-destruction/risk-taking

The obvious dangers of unwise or excessive drug use have led to speculation that sometimes drug taking is prompted by self-destructive impulses. Alcohol dependence, for example, has been called 'chronic suicide'. This theory is compatible with the fact that many institutionalised drugtakers appear to have poor self-images and sometimes have quite strong feelings of hostility directed at themselves. It is also consistent with the fact that some drugtakers, for whatever reasons, do overdose on psychoactive substances. Another theory is that drug use is a form of risk-taking. But there is little evidence that drugtakers are particularly predisposed to take risks. Even so, it does appear that some individuals probably choose drugs which produce effects compatible with their personalities or emotional needs.

Resolution of personal problems

Clinical studies indicate that many drug dependent people have serious personal problems. In addition, youthful illegal drug use is often a symbolic gesture of defiance against parental or authority values. It is also possible that adopting the lifestyle of the drugtaker (or the 'regular' at the local) provides some people with friendship and social support. There is little doubt that strong social pressures exist, encouraging individuals to conform to certain patterns of drug use as part of more general lifestyles. As ever though, it is difficult to 'work backwards' and deduce whether an individual's current drug use is attributable to pre-existing poor social relationships.

Environmental approaches

Environmental approaches relate drug use to wider social and cultural factors. Many studies have examined the life experiences of drugtakers, emphasising issues such as broken homes, delinquency, educational and occupational disadvantages. It has also been suggested that social changes or deprivation sometimes precipitate or foster drug use. The following section examines some of these envi-

2

2

ronmental factors.

Family disturbance

Much attention has been focused on the family background of drugtakers, especially of drug dependent individuals in treatment institutions. Many studies of
such clinic populations have noted that a high proportion have come from abnormal or disturbed homes and that excessive drug use or drug dependence does
sometimes appear to have been aggravated by a family problem of some sort.

The suggested link between drug misuse and parental separation or other family disruptions becomes far less clear-cut when drugtakers are compared to other
people. There is no clear evidence that drugtakers *do* differ in this respect from
non-drugtakers. In addition, surveys provide abundant evidence that the majority
of casual or experimental drug users do not come from disturbed homes.

There is evidence, however, that many institutionalised drug dependants
(including problem drinkers) report having parents who were themselves alcohol
or drug misusers or who were otherwise unhappy or disturbed. It is widely noted
that institutionalised drug dependants often come from 'loveless homes' or have
been 'excessively protected'. A result of this appears to be the limited abilities of
some of these individuals to form satisfactory relationships or to communicate
with other people. There is little doubt that very often one generation will imitate
the drug use of their predecessors. Parents who use drugs excessively may well
produce children who do the same, even if they do so with substances of which
their parents strongly disapprove, such as cannabis or heroin.

Unemployment, education and work problems

There is abundant and convincing evidence that many institutionalised young
drugtakers exhibit signs of educational disturbance, particularly truancy. In addition many 'drop out' of further or higher education or have had very poor
employment records. In fact, a growing body of evidence suggests that illegal drug
use in the United Kingdom is associated with unemployment. In contrast, tobacco
use has clearly declined as unemployment has risen. Young unemployed people
appear to be particularly susceptible to illegal drugs, but the relationship between
drugs and unemployment is complex and requires further research.

Social class

Drug taking and drug dependence occur at all social levels. Illegal drug use in
America has often been connected with severe social deprivation, for example
among poor urban ghetto dwellers. A similar picture has developed in some
deprived areas of Britain. Despite this, drug users are drawn from all social classes
– in fact, a recent national survey found that the higher socio-economic groups
were the most prominent in drug usage.[1]

The youthfulness of many drugtakers implies that few will have attained their
final occupational level. Even so, many surveys have shown that experimental
drug use is quite common among students (who are predominantly from non-

manual backgrounds). Social class also appears to influence patterns of drug use. It has been suggested that drug users from working class backgrounds are more likely to be heavy or excessive users of a wide range of drugs. Those from middle class families are generally more restrained and selective.

Peer pressure

One of the most commonly given reasons for initial drug use is peer pressure – being goaded into it by friends and acquaintances – and a very large number of studies support this view. This appears to be as applicable to heroin injectors as to cannabis smokers. Some young people appear to be especially likely to be subject to social pressures to indulge in drug use. These include the unemployed, people whose jobs encourage drinking or students and others living away from their parental homes. All are likely to be exposed to, if not influenced by, the fashions and enthusiasms of their peers. Sometimes this pressure will generate strong social endorsement for using cannabis, LSD or heroin.

There is plentiful evidence to support the view that peer pressure is often a potent reason for beginning or continuing drug use. This conclusion rests largely upon self-reporting by drug users who may be reluctant to concede that their use was motivated by any 'abnormal' causes. It is also possible that disturbed or impressionable individuals may be particularly susceptible to peer pressure. This is consistent with the frequently expressed criticism that drug use is sometimes due to 'falling into bad company'. The fact is that from the drug user's point of view the company is often very good. It is clear that people will normally only be influenced by those who they like and wish to be accepted by. There is very little evidence to support the view, beloved of certain tabloid newspapers, that innocent children are lured on to the rocks of addiction by commercially motivated pushers lurking outside the nursery.

Ideology

Some types of drug use are much more widely accepted and indulged in than others. Alcohol and tobacco are generally seen as symbols of maturity and sociability. Medically prescribed tranquillisers and sleeping pills are not seen in this way, and their use is much less discussed or publicly paraded. And finally, illegal drugs carry a whole 'belief system' with them, often regarded as being indicative of protest against or rejection of conventional attitudes and values.

During the 1960s drug use, especially that of cannabis and LSD, was widely linked with the emergence of a distinctive 'teenage culture' associated in the public mind with permissiveness and hedonism. 'Turn on, tune in, drop out' and other slogans clearly linked drugs with the hippy movement and with a variety of 'new' religious cults.

There is a clear relationship between religious ideology and the use of illegal drugs. Self-reports by young drugtakers, especially those deeply involved with drug use, showed that during the 1960s and 1970s most regarded themselves as not sharing their parents' religious views. It could be that the very illegality of

2

2

drugs frightens off people with conventional and orthodox beliefs. It certainly seems that strong religious views may 'insulate' young people from experimenting with illegal drugs. Religion certainly appears to influence alcohol use and is often a reason why people choose not to drink at all. This applies not only to Islamic countries but also to parts of Scotland and to large areas of the United States.

Delinquency

Many institutionalised drug dependants have criminal records preceding their drug use. This is also true of institutionalised problem drinkers. As noted above, any type of unusual or anti-social behaviour may predispose those indulging in it to break other social conventions. For this reason people who have a criminal history may be more prepared to begin using illegal drugs than would others. In addition some of the factors which foster illegal drug use may be the same as those prompting other types of crime. In spite of this, the overwhelming majority of those using illegal drugs are not otherwise delinquent.

Occupation

Some professions certainly expose people to distinctive social pressures and other stresses. Those in medical, nursing and associated occupations have long been known to be at high risk of becoming drug dependent. Until the 'post-war boom' of youthful heroin use, virtually the only people known to be dependent on opiates in Britain were those in professions which gave them ready access to drugs (usually morphine) or individuals who had become drug dependent while undergoing medical treatment. Doctors have also widely been reported to have high rates of alcohol problems. It is important to remember that the medical profession is relatively well informed about the effects of drugs – calling into question the view that drug problems arise from a lack of knowledge.

Availability

To a large extent, specific drugs are used because they are available. Most social groups use whatever substances they have ready access to. Many young drug users, particularly those in treatment institutions, appear to be willing to use whatever is to hand. Not everyone is so catholic in their drug tastes. Even so it has often been noted that when, for any reason, large amounts of a drug are available at a reasonable price from whatever source, their use and misuse will invariably increase. The extent of alcohol and tobacco use, for instance, is certainly related to their high levels of availability. There is also abundant evidence that the consumption of any drug, be it heroin or alcohol, is influenced by its price relative to other drugs.

Studies of drug users show that whatever their previous characteristics and inclinations, the availability of drugs in conducive surroundings is an important reason for initial use. The upsurge in drug use which began in the 1960s has been attributed in large measure to the introduction of new drug types, either because they had just been 'invented' or because they were being imported from other countries. The fashion for using amphetamines recreationally was certainly encouraged by the vast quantities available either through thefts or through prescription. In addition the upsurge in heroin use in the 1960s and 1970s was clearly exacerbated by casual prescribing so that 'spare' supplies could be passed on to others eager to experiment.

As the above should have hinted, the National Health Service is one of the major suppliers of drugs in Britain. Prescribed drugs have certainly been re-sold, stolen or just left around for others to take. Some of those receiving prescriptions have accidentally become 'therapeutically dependent' upon opiates, barbiturates, tranquillisers and other substances. It is clear that even drugs which are considered to be relatively 'safe', such as Ativan, Librium and Valium, will be misused provided that they are available in sufficient quantities.

The medical profession has frequently tried to deal with this 'leakage'. The famous 'Ipswich Experiment', when doctors voluntarily curtailed amphetamine prescribing, proved beyond doubt that controlling the supply of drugs may sometimes drastically reduce their misuse. Such restrictions will, of course, only work if the demand for such drugs is comparatively low and if no alternative sources of supply exist. The classic western example of an attempt to control the availability of a drug was Prohibition in the United States (1920-33). During this period, while 'conventional' alcohol-related problems such as liver cirrhosis declined dramatically, others emerged in the form of bootlegging and gangsterism. Even in Britain today it is clear that curtailing a wide range of drug use requires considerable Customs, police, court and penal resources. In addition, restricting the legitimate supply of any drug creates the risk that illicit supplies may be sought instead. These may be poorly manufactured, adulterated or impure. Furthermore, infringements on civil liberties and the imposition of harsh penalties may cause more harm than the drugs themselves would otherwise do.

Historical reasons

There has been considerable discussion about why certain types of drug use, especially recreational drug use, blossom when they do. Very often the explanations are clear cut – the introduction of tobacco to Britain by Sir Walter Raleigh or the production of new drugs by the pharmaceutical industry. More often than not though, explanations are hard to pin down – the emergence of a distinctive youth drug culture during the 1950s and 1960s occurred for a myriad of reasons, many of which remain only partly understood.

It has been noted that even during the 1940s and earlier, a certain amount of drug trafficking was carried out by sailors. Cannabis use also received a boost from American musicians and 'beat' poets. Even so, there is little to suggest that either of these influences went much beyond the dockyard gates or the fringes of the avant-garde. The arrival of West Indian immigrants to Britain during the 1950s certainly introduced for the first time fairly large numbers of people used to smoking cannabis. Some of these immigrants certainly continued their cannabis smoking, but it is difficult to see them actively influencing the host community.

2

2

That said, while immigrant cannabis use was probably fairly self-contained, it may have contributed to the general spread of the recreational use of 'new' drugs. It is also probable that, like many other fashions from wearing jeans to break dancing, certain types of drug use were adopted due to American influence.

The whole lifestyle of young adults changed during the 1960s. Pop music, 'permissiveness' and 'hippy culture' arrived, and drugs were legitimised by cult figures and the new generation of millionaire rock superstars in the 1970s. Youth culture was established with a heavy emphasis on rebellion against established norms. Invariably the drugs used complemented the musical preferences of the user, which was often explicitly drug-oriented. Amphetamines fuelled the Northern soul circuit, helping dancers stay awake all night, while cannabis soothed the strains of softer sounds and LSD helped the listener appreciate Pink Floyd. With the demise of the hippy, came the nihilism of punk with its glue and heroin. More recently, dance has made a comeback, with the rave introducing a raft of new 'feel-good' drugs such as ecstasy.

Many people (politicians and newspaper editors among them) make the simplistic assumption that drug use is caused by the activities of traffickers and dealers. In fact, most studies conclude that initial drug use is largely attributable to encouragement by friends. The direct influence of commercially motivated suppliers has almost certainly been over-emphasised. In more general terms there is a great deal of evidence supporting the view that young people's drug use largely spreads in a friendly and hospitable way, reflecting much wider social changes. That said, drug use is fostered both by demand and supply and as noted by Freemantle[2] the international drug trade is a massive and relentlessly expanding industry.

The increase in officially recorded drug dependence may be a logical corollary of the growing acceptance of all forms of drug use. Because relatively large numbers of people were prepared to experiment with substances such as cannabis and LSD in the 1960s, a minority may have been encouraged to use opiates. Even so, such a conclusion is by no means certain and the great majority of illegal drug users appear to confine themselves to casual experimentation.

Sociological theories

Several sociological theories have been applied to the post-war spread of drugs in Britain. Probably the most important views are that drug use reflects an increase in *alienation* or *anomie*. Such theories attribute drug use to new social pressures, such as competition for jobs, housing and education. Those whose needs are left unmet by the mainstream of society simply opt out, turning instead to the supportive 'alternative' lifestyle of the drug scene. This provides status and companionship without the demands of the mundane, workaday world. Instead of having to accept the constraints of 'straight' society, with its long-term planning and deferment of gratification, the drug scene permits instant enjoyment. Because of its free and easy values, the scene allows people to 'do their own thing' and becomes a haven for individuals who, for whatever reasons, cannot or will not fit into the rat race of the broader society. This view certainly makes some sense of the commitment to drug taking. It is also consistent with the fact that many drug dependent people have psychological problems or are socially deprived. In particular this approach has the merit of linking drug use with the structure of society.

Another sociological view is that once a 'deviant' behaviour, such as drug taking, becomes evident society attempts to control it and inadvertently makes it worse. The logic of this theory is that as drug taking is labelled and legislated against, those who indulge in it become more secretive and more cut off – their deviance is 'amplified'. Consequently, the social controls against this 'growing' problem are increased which, in turn, ratchets the deviants into further isolation and so on. This theory provides a useful insight into the possible effects of identifying and attempting to curb a newly defined social problem. There is much truth in this view and some drugtakers certainly appear to enjoy the drama conferred upon their activities by legislation and by their battles against those who enforce it.

As this chapter has attempted to show, many plausible theories have been put forward to explain why people use drugs and why some become dependent upon them. Each of these theories is consistent with the characteristics of some drugtakers, but it is clear that no single theory can account for all types of drug use. Drug taking and drug dependence appear to be influenced by a great number of factors, whether constitutional, individual or environmental. Probably different reasons account for different types of drug use. The casual or experimental use of drugs is probably due largely to social pressures combined with availability. Dependence upon drugs may well be attributable to much more profound factors such as social deprivation or psychological disturbance. And finally, other factors may account for the way some people remain dependent while others do not.

1. Ramsay M and Partidge S (1999) *Drug Misuse Declared in 1998: Results from the British Crime Survey*, London: Home Office.
2. Freemantle B (1985) *The Fix*, London: Michael Joseph.

2

how
many drug users
are **there?**

3

TEXT | **GARY HAYES**

YOUR | QUESTIONS | **ANSWERED**

What drug using figures do we have and

what do they say (and not say)? | Who and how many people use drugs? | Which

types of drugs do people use? | How much do drugs cost? | Where do today's

drugs come from? | How many prisoners use drugs? | How many people

experience health problems due to drug use? | How many people are addicted to

drugs? | How many people are in treatment? | How many people die

from drug use?

3

This chapter answers questions most often asked about illegal drugs: how many people use drugs and how many are hurt by drugs. Statistics on the prevalence of drug use and the number of people seeking help for their drug use are described, and an attempt is made to explain what these figures say, and more importantly, what they don't say.

What do the statistics say?

DrugScope deals daily with enquiries on prevalence, or the extent, of drug use in the UK. The answer, unfortunately, is never straightforward. The most accurate statistics are taken from a number of population samples. The statistics are based on a number of important assumptions, however, and these must be fully acknowledged before any figures are used.

Proportionately representative of population

Who the researchers select for surveying is important. Two factors must be considered:

- the sample questioned must be representative of the general population as a whole
- they must be selected fairly, either randomly or matched to the population.

For example, if, out of a group of 1,000 adults from a wide range of ages, ethnic groups, religions, gender, social classes (the list can go on), 200 say they have used a drug at least once, we could predict that, with all things equal, this figure could be applied to the rest of the population. We would therefore say that 20 per cent of the adult population have tried a drug at least once.

However, because drug use is illicit, it is difficult to survey accurately. Users are often marginalised and difficult to reach. Most large scale surveys, such as the British Crime Survey, distribute questionnaires to people's homes, using the Postcode Address File (selecting people from a postcode database), thereby omitting large numbers of people who do not live in homes or have recognised addresses, such as those living in care or on the streets. Such surveys, therefore, run the risk of underestimating the overall level of drug use by excluding people possibly more likely to use drugs.

Robustness (validity and reliability, bias)

For figures to be robust they must be:

- valid –that we are measuring what we are supposed to be measuring
- reliable – that the figures are accurately and consistently measured
- unbiased –that the measurements are not consistently higher or lower than the true value.

Robustness can be affected by two main factors: how people are questioned and human nature.

How people are questioned

An important consideration is who, how and when people are questioned. A teacher asking children at school about their drug use may get a very different answer than if an unknown researcher at the local youth club asks them the same question. Researchers must consider literacy when using questionnaires: if a respondent cannot read or write, or finds it difficult, the chances are they will not fill in a questionnaire.

Human nature

People often lie, particularly about behaviour which is either frowned upon or given prestige. Parents, teachers, managers, for example, may be inclined to deny that they have used a drug, whereas a student may be eager to admit using drugs if it is regarded as fashionable at their college.

How can we test robustness?

There are ways of gauging whether a respondent is answering accurately and reliably. One way is to repeat a question, but in a different way. Another is to ask a question to which you know the answer. If the question is answered wrongly, a respondent's accuracy can be tested and even measured. Some questionnaires, for example, add a bogus drug to the list of drugs being surveyed. The number of responses stating 'yes' they have used this bogus drug, can indicate the level of accuracy among respondents. Another way is to carry out drug tests, which can establish fairly accurately the existence of a drug in someone's body. Again, this can be used to establish how accurately an individual has responded to questioning or to measure rates of (recent) drug use.

What the surveys say

The best source of data on young people's drug use is the British Crime Survey (BCS), which covers England and Wales, and the parallel Scottish and Northern Irish Crime Surveys. Although their differing methodologies do not allow for direct comparisons or merging, this is often inevitable. The following section is a summary of these and other main UK drug prevalence studies.

British Crime Survey

The British Crime Survey (BCS) is the largest household survey in England and Wales on experiences of crime, including the use of drugs. Because of its size, the rigour of its methodology and the fact that it has been running since 1982, it is regarded as the most reliable drug prevalence survey for the UK and hence sets the recognised baseline figures for drug prevalence.

Coverage

Contrary to what the name suggests, it does not cover all of Britain, nor because of its size and scope, does it break down in any detail the behaviour of specific

3

3

groups or minorities.

Sample
The sample is derived from the Postcode Address File, which selects households for surveying. The sample ranges in age from 16 to 59 years. Many parts of the survey report on the main age group of drug users in the UK, the under 30s, often highlighting otherwise hidden patterns in drug using aetiology.

How often is it done?
The BCS is carried out biennially, allowing trends to be monitored every two years.

What does it report?
The BCS is useful in providing breakdowns of drug use according to age, region, ethnicity, socio-economic status, drug type and levels of use according to recall periods – such as use in last month, last year and ever (lifetime).

How useful are recall periods?
Different drug use recall periods are useful for ascertaining which drugs are currently being used. The categorisation can also be used to help differentiate between regular and experimental use. An individual who has used a drug in the last month is likely to be a current user – though not always. It is important, therefore, to recognise that the number of people who have ever tried a drug, or indeed have taken a drug recently, is not an indicator of current use. Most people who try a drug, do just that – try it and then stop.

The BCS main findings
In 1998, roughly 10,000 16-59-year-olds were questioned using Computer Assisted Personal Interviewing, where respondents key their answers into a laptop computer. This has been shown to make answering easier and to encourage honest responses (see *British Crime Survey 1994* for an explanation).

Overall prevalence
Nearly all the BCS surveys since they began have shown a steady increase in overall drug use, particularly in the category of "lifetime" use or "ever tried" a drug. The 1998 BCS reported around one in three (32 per cent) adults ever having used a drug, 11 per cent within the last year and 6 per cent within the last month. Table 3.1 shows the steady increase in ever having used a drug, from the last three surveys.

Table 3.1 | **Prevalence for 16–59-year-olds, 1994 to 1998 in percentages**

	1994	**1996**	**1998**
Ever tried	28	29	32
Within the last year	10	10	11
Within the last month	6	6	6

Source: Home Office, *British Crime Survey,* 1998.

Who is using?
Young adults
The years around the end of compulsory schooling at 16 years and the approach of middle age are consistently found to be times of greatest drug consumption, with peak years particularly among the 16- to 24-year-olds.[1]

Of the adults surveyed by the BCS, the highest lifetime use rates (at 55 per cent)were among 20-24-year-olds. This is followed by the 16-19-year-olds (49 per cent) and the 25-29 age group (45 per cent).

Therefore, roughly half of the under 30s in the survey have at some point in their lives tried an illicit substance. As Figure 3.1 shows, the trend for lifetime use is steadily upwards, for the under 30s, with rates of use rising from 43 per cent in 1994 to 45 and 49 per cent in 1996 and 1998 respectively.

Among the under 30s as a whole, drug use prevalence tends to outstrip that of the older generation by at least 2:1 (49 per cent of 16-29 year olds, for example,

Figure 3.1 | **Lifetime use for 16-29 year olds**

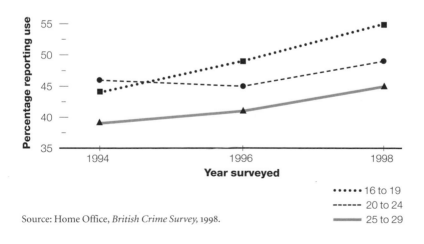

Source: Home Office, *British Crime Survey,* 1998.

• • • • • 16 to 19
‐ ‐ ‐ ‐ ‐ 20 to 24
━━━ 25 to 29

3

3

have tried a drug, compared with 25 per cent of 30 to 59 year olds). This becomes more pronounced when prevalence rates for regular use are looked at (16 per cent compared to 3 per cent having used any drug within the last month respectively).

Where do they use?
Regional variations

The prevalence figures from the BCS apply to England and Wales only. A regional breakdown is given where obvious trends emerge, but figures are not detailed for each drug nor are all recall periods and ages given. Figures focus on the under 30s, who are more inclined to use drugs and so more likely to significantly reveal trends.

Prevalence rates are highest in south-east England and in London, a trend which in the past has been spreading elsewhere.[2] Although waning, London still has the highest rates for drug use in England and Wales. For example, among the 16-29 year olds, 32 per cent reported in 1998 using any drug within the last year, compared to 17 per cent in Wales, 19 per cent in Anglia, 21 per cent in the Midlands, 26 per cent in the north and 25 per cent (the national average) in the south.

Care with these figures should be taken as drug use tends to be localised. A number of good regional surveys show a large degree of variation across regions and within them.

Figure 3.2 | **Use of any drug in the last year for 16–29 year olds**

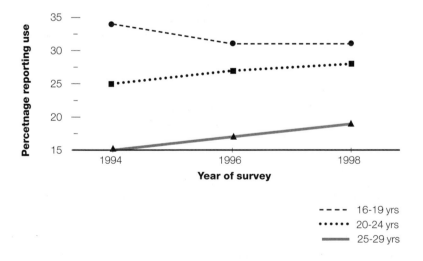

What drugs do people use?

The BCS provides data on who is using which type of drug, and when – this is very useful for understanding which drugs are moving in or out of fashion.

Cannabis is the most commonly used illegal drug, with roughly a quarter of the whole survey, and 40 per cent of 16-19-year-olds, reporting having ever taken it. Amphetamines, poppers and hallucinogens are next in order. What is interesting is the relative popularity these drugs have among what is often termed the clubbing generation, the 19-24-year-olds. Of these, roughly one in five have used amphetamine and one in ten ecstasy or LSD. The fact that the rates for use in the last month is half that of lifetime use, indicates that a very large proportion are using more regularly.

The BCS is a poor indicator of the patterns of prevalence of the so-called hard drugs. With only one per cent of the BCS sample reporting use of heroin or crack, the data set is too small to reveal any significant changes in patterns of use. Cocaine use on the other hand, at three per cent of the whole sample and six per cent of the under 30s ever having used, has shown a steady increase since 1992, particularly among the under 30s in London.

What does the BCS not say?

As mentioned above, the BCS does not cover Scotland or Northern Ireland. It also omits those under 16 or over 60 years of age. Furthermore, because it is a household survey, the BCS omits those not living in recognised household accommodation. As a crime survey carried out by the Home Office, the BCS is likely to receive under-reporting of drug use. Unlike reporting a crime that has happened to the respondent, the drugs questionnaire asks respondents to reveal illegal activities they themselves have perpetrated. The recall periods although useful, are not a reliable indicator of regular or current use. These factors would suggest that the BCS is liable to underestimate drug use.

Other important surveys
Health Education Monitoring Survey (HEMS)[3]

This is the 1997 survey of 4,314 adults aged 16-74 in England, carried out by Social Survey Division of the Office of National Statistics (ONS) on behalf of the Health Education Authority (HEA) as a follow-up to the 1995 survey. The HEMS survey looked at a range of health-related behaviours, including patterns of tobacco smoking and alcohol and illicit drug consumption. The findings are similar to the BCS, revealing, for example, that 27 per cent of 16-29 year olds reported use within the last year.

Drug Realities[4]

The 1996 Drug Realities Survey builds on the results of the earlier 1995 Drug Realities Survey, giving the extent of self-reported drug use among 4,647 11-35

3

3

year olds in England in 1996. The survey looks at personal drug use prevalence, patterns of use, attitudes, and other related behaviours. It should be noted that although useful, part of the 1996 sample was a quota sample and part random probability sample[5] (similar to the BCS) which did not have a high response rate – possibly biasing the results. The 1996 survey revealed that 23 per cent of its 11-35 year old sample reported using a drug in the last year and 12 per cent in the last month.

Scottish Crime Survey

The Scottish Crime Survey (SCS) uses different methods of research than the BCS, making direct comparisons difficult. However, Scottish surveys generally reveal that young adults (aged 16-30) are more likely to have used a drug than their English or Welsh counterparts, while the over-30s are less inclined. In the 1996 SCS, 3,175 people were given questionnaires asking about their drug use.[6] Responses showed a more sustained and general increase in drug use, with lifetime use rising from just over 18 per cent in 1993 to nearly 23 per cent in 1996. Use within the last year also rose from 7 per cent in 1993 to 9 per cent in 1996. While these figures are generally lower than those for England and Wales, and do not display the levelling out found there, the difference between lifetime use and use in the last year is perhaps less pronounced in Scotland than for the rest of the UK: two in five (rather than one in three) Scots who have ever taken drugs are still doing so.

Northern Ireland Survey

In 1999 a report on adults' knowledge and awareness of illicit drugs was published, using information from the Northern Ireland Omnibus survey of 977 people carried out in February 1997.[7] The main findings indicated that approximately 27 per cent of those aged 16 to 59 years reported that they had ever taken an illicit drug, slightly less than the figure given for the same ages by the BCS (at 32 per cent).

Who is using what – a more detailed analysis

The crime surveys are useful because they give a baseline figure of use among the general adult population. However, drug use differs greatly across the population, often localised and specific to certain ages, class or lifestyles – something a large, generic survey fails to pick up. The following section looks at surveys conducted among specific groups of users.

Schoolchildren

The oldest and largest survey of drug taking by school children is conducted bi-annually by John Balding of the Schools Health Unit in Exeter. This chapter draws on two other large scale surveys: the Drug Realities survey and the *Health Behaviour in School-aged Children, whose methods are more* rigorous than those of the Balding survey.

John Balding's school survey (Young People in 1997, 1999 etc)
Balding's studies consistently survey the largest number of schoolchildren in Britain – 28,756 in 1997.[8] The Schools Health Unit in Exeter (SHUE) databases contain data from a large number of independent surveys carried out across the country using the SHUE survey methods mainly by health authorities, in collaboration with other local partners. These partnerships are responsible for the timing and sampling procedures, although there is a strong incentive to make the sample representative of their own area. The sampling is therefore not random nor fully representative. School teachers known to the class collect data in these surveys. The SHUE believes, rightly or wrongly, that this promotes a conducive atmosphere in the classroom, and with the support of classroom assistants, the completion rate of pupils with special educational needs is increased.

It is estimated that on any given day about 10 per cent of pupils are absent from school. Although drug users may be more likely to play truant, absent pupils may also include groups like those who are often ill and those frightened to go to school, who may be less likely to use drugs than the rest of the class. The effect of absentees on the assessment of prevalence rates is not known. That said, the survey results are remarkably similar to those generated by studies with more rigorous sampling methods. The size of the samples and availability of data stretching back for over a decade make the Balding studies a uniquely useful source. For the purposes of this chapter, we will make use of the 1997 survey and some of the skeleton figures from the 1999 survey.[9]

Health Behaviour in School-aged Children (HBSC)[10]
Another survey carried out by the HEA, the HBSC forms part of a cross-national survey of young people's lifestyles in 24 European countries. The first survey was carried out in 1995, the second 1997, questioning 10,407 pupils aged 11 to 15 years across England, of which the 14 to 15 year olds were asked about drugs.

Drug Realities
See page 47 above.

Use begins at fourteen
Even among school children there is a very strong variation in drug using behaviour. All the surveys carried out in this group, reveal a watershed around the age of 13 to 14 years of age. Those under that age are unlikely to have tried drugs, those above likely.

In 1996 around 16 per cent of 11-14 year olds in the Drug Realities survey reported ever taking drugs or misusing solvents. This sharply rises for the older school children to around 40 per cent for 14-16 year olds (as reported in the Balding survey) – see Figure 3.3.

3

3

Figure 3.3 | **Percentage of 11–16 year olds who have ever used a drug**

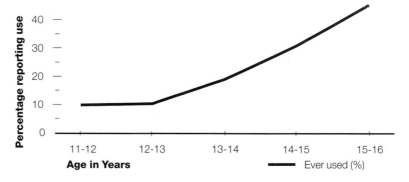

Source: Balding 1998

More recent use

For the first time, the 1997 Balding survey questioned regular use of drugs, revealing that up to the age of 13, between 1 and 2 per cent use drugs regularly. Nearly 2 per cent of 11-12 year olds reported using within the last year, and 1 per cent in the last month. This begins to rise steeply from the age of 13 onwards.

The survey shows that roughly 7 per cent of 13-14 year olds had used a drug in the last month, rising to 13 per cent for 14-15 year olds and 20 per cent for 15-16 year olds. The Drug Realities survey, although it does not provide the same age breakdowns, supports these findings, reporting 1 per cent of 11-14 year olds and 12 per cent of 14-16 year olds having used a drug in the last year. In essence, this would suggest that about half 14-15 year olds, for example, with any drug experience will have used within the last month.

School age use falling

The 1999 Balding survey suggests an overall decline in drug use, particularly cannabis. For the third year running, the prevalence rates among 15-16 year olds fell, from 32 per cent in 1996 to 21 per cent in 1999 (see Figure 3.4). The authors, originally attributing the initial drop to a lower average age, confirm that this fall is on-going but give no explanation.

Many contributory factors are possible, such as drop in availability, changes in fashion and lifestyle choices, and the role of demand reduction activities, such as education. As figures for drug seizures and police reports indicate that drug availability is actually on the increase, it is reasonable to conclude that young people are simply choosing not to take drugs. The BCS, the first to show a decline in young people's use in 1996, revealed a fall in ecstasy use and a rise in alcohol and cocaine use in London, marking a change in drug of choice for many in this area.

Put simply, school children, it appears, are setting their own trend, and choosing not to follow that set by previous generations.

Figure 3.4 | **Rise and fall in lifetime prevalence among 12–13 and 14–15 year olds**

Lifetime prevalence

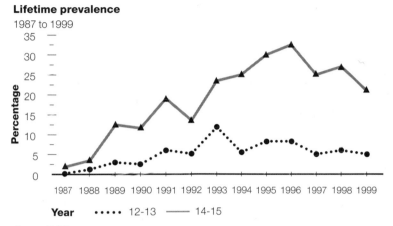

Source: Balding 1988, 2000

Class and lifestyle

Until recently there was a strongly-held view that socio-economic status is in some way related to drug use. This view, however, has been challenged. The BCS has consistently found that people living in households where the head was in a non-manual occupation had higher levels of lifetime use than those living in 'manual households'. However, while those with household incomes of over £30,000 tended to have high lifetime use, those with incomes of under £5,000 had the highest lifetime use. Of the young unemployed, 40 per cent had used a drug in the last year, compared with 25 per cent of those in employment.

Leisure drug use and the social life associated with it, are often the preserve of those who can afford to do so. The 1998 BCS found that those living in rising areas according to the ACORN classification,[11] are roughly twice as likely to have used a drug in the last year and month than people from most other categories. Rising areas are characterised by young employed, urban dwellers –the group most likely to go to pubs and clubs.[12]

Problematic or heavy use

Problematic or heavy drug users tend to be long-term economically inactive, living with their parents or partner, and living in urban or suburban areas (as the Scottish Drug Misuse Database reveals). However, recent research in England has

3

3

shown that the use of heroin, often associated with problematic use, is spreading into more mainstream groups of young people.[13] Heroin is not only becoming cheaper but is also being sold in smaller, smokable quantities to young people in rural and urban areas, the majority of whom are in full- or part-time employment and successful relationships.

Clubbing

Lifestyle is a very high predictor of drug use in some circumstances. Studies by Release[14] and the London School of Hygiene and Tropical Medicine[15] have revealed the close link between drug use and clubbing. Some of the highest prevalence rates for any group have been found among clubbers, with 99 per cent of 200 clubbers reporting having ever used a drug, and 93 per cent planning to use that night. Different drugs are specific to particular dance events and music. For example, while 73 per cent of the sample attending a Techno night were planning to take ecstasy, only 40 per cent of those at a Garage night were planning to do so.

Figure 3.5 | **Extent of drug use at different dance events**

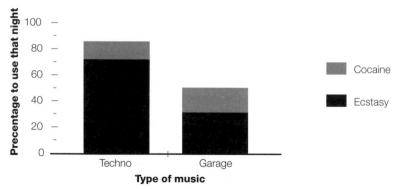

Source: Release 1997

Homeless people

Homeless people are difficult to survey, mainly because they are difficult to contact using conventional methods. However, there are a few, small-scale surveys that have looked at levels of drug use among this group, and found it to be very prevalent. A small survey in 1996 carried out in London found that at least 88 per cent of young homeless people use at least one drug regularly.[16] A later study carried out in Leicester asked homeless people of all ages (16-60) whether they had used a drug. Many were in temporary accommodation and not sleeping rough as in the 1996 London study. This found that 42 per cent, nearly all of whom were male, were using some type of drug. Predictably, a large percentage (33 per cent), were using cannabis, followed by 12.5 per cent who were using heroin. On the basis of these findings, it can be concluded that surveys that fail to include groups such as the homeless, particularly if they are local surveys in an area with many homeless people, will underestimate the level of drug use.

Figure 3.6 | **Current drug use among a small sample of Leicester homeless**

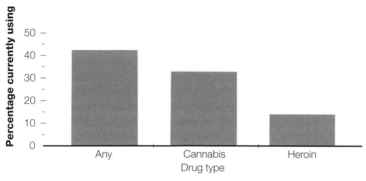

Source: Flemen 1997

Drug use in prison

There is a strongly-documented link between drug taking and acquisitive crime. In an attempt to understand this link and, where possible, break it, the government has undertaken a number of initiatives, two of which try to ascertain levels of drug use among arrestees and detainees. The first, a large-scale pilot survey known as NEW-ADAM, scans arrestees for drug use using questionnaires and drug tests. The second, known as Mandatory Drug Testing (MDT), randomly and routinely tests prisoners while in detention. Because of their size and use of drug tests, these surveys offer a very reliable and valid estimate of drug use among these groups, provided inmates do not find ways of cheating the tests – which many have.

Again, the data should be analysed carefully. While a test may show the presence of a drug in a detainee's blood, it reveals nothing of how often the user takes that drug, how much nor, in the case of cannabis, which can stay in the body for up to a month, how long ago it was used (see Chapter 11).

Arrestees

On the whole, drug use has been found to be very high among inmates – particularly on entry. Three in five arrestees (61 per cent) screened by NEW-ADAM tested positive for at least one drug, and over a quarter (27 per cent) for two or more drugs.[17] It should be borne in mind that half of the positive tests were for cannabis, which, as well as possibly remaining in the body for several weeks, is not linked, as is heroin, to crime. It was found that those who linked their arrest to

3

3

their drug use were more likely to have tested positive for a number of drugs, typically crack and heroin, indicating that heavy or problematic drug use is linked to crime rather than drug use per se (see Chapter 5 for a discussion of drugs and crime).

Inmates
Contrary to common belief, drug use, particularly of cocaine and heroin, drops once the user is in detention. Mandatory Drug Testing shows that roughly one in five inmates, when tested randomly, test positive for drugs. Not surprisingly, cannabis accounts for nearly all positive results, with only around 5 per cent testing positive for opiates. Benzodiazepines are found in small but significant quantities (2 per cent), particularly among women.

Other prison surveys
Other, more conventional, surveys have shown a higher proportion of drug use than testing appears to reveal. This adds some credence to concerns that prisoners are findings ways to avoid testing positive, such as switching from cannabis, with its long residual retention, to drugs which are excreted much more quickly from the body – eg, heroin. The surveys mentioned below provide details on levels of use, injecting and measures of drug use problems in prisons.

Figure 3.7 | **Urine test results among arrestees**

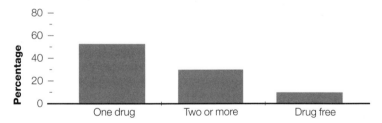

Source: Bennett, 1998

A study by the ONS[18] revealed that half of the male remand prisoners showed some signs of problematic drug use – eg, 40 per cent showed severe symptoms of dependence. Of female remand prisoners, 54 per cent showed some signs of problematic drug use, with 47 per cent assessed as severely dependent. Sentenced prisoners were slightly less likely to show such signs of dependence: with 43 per cent of men and 42 per cent of women showing moderate to severe signs of dependence.

Among male remand prisoners, 38 per cent reported having used drugs during their current time in prison, as did 48 per cent of male sentenced prisoners. Women were less likely to report drug use during their term, with a quarter of remand and a third (34 per cent) of sentenced prisoners reporting use.

The most prevalent drug was cannabis, followed by heroin – whose use was reported by roughly a fifth of male and female sentenced prisoners. One in five of the men reporting use, claim they started using in prison.

Although reported injecting prior to imprisonment was fairly high (17 per cent of male remand and 28 per cent of female remand had ever injected), this fell sharply once inside, with only 2 per cent reporting injecting during their present term.

Young offenders

Less is known about drug use among young offenders. The only major study, carried out by the Home Office,[19] found that among 16 to 20 year old arrestees, 11 per cent tested positive for opiates, and 5 per cent cocaine. Another study,[20] this time using interviews, found that 65 per cent said they had used cannabis, a quarter amphetamine, and over one fifth ecstasy. While these figures tell us that young offenders as far more likely to have used a drug, they say nothing about use by young offenders while in detention.

How many people are hurt by drug use?

Prevalence figures indicate the number of people using drugs but say little about the effects drugs have on individuals and society. The effect which generates most interest is harm, particularly among academics, health professionals and politicians – those who usually carry out and commission research. Harm is generally categorised into four areas:

- addiction
- health (morbidity)
- drug-related deaths (mortality)
- accidents.

Addiction

Addiction or problematic use is a difficult concept to survey. Those with drug-related problems tend to be difficult to find, and addiction is difficult to measure. Experts consistently fail to agree on what constitutes an addict, problematic use or problematic user. What to one person is a manageable activity can be seen by others as problematic. While the debate goes on, estimates as to how many people are experiencing drug problems have to be pooled from a number of sources, using a range of criteria – none of which measure addiction directly or comprehensively.

Regional Drug Misuse Database

The main source for a measure of problematic drug users are the Regional Drug Misuse Databases (RDMDs). In essence, the RDMDs log the number of people seeking new help for their drug use. The database, therefore, counts not the num-

3

3

ber of people addicted to a drug, but those who use drugs and seek help.

The Department of Health (DoH), which reproduces the national data, states that the figures reveal only the number of individuals with problem drug use presenting to RDMD-participating services for the first time within a six-month period. The data, in other words, is not submitted by all agencies and so is not comprehensive. It gives only the number of new, not ongoing, treatments.
One temptation is to join the two biannual figures to create an annual figure. Due to possible double counting however, ie when an individual seeks new treatment in consecutive periods, this is not possible. The RDMD data is useful because it is both ongoing – biannually, and large scale, covering England, Wales and Scotland. An RDMD is planned for Northern Ireland.

Estimating the number of addicts in treatment

While the data on new notifications helps track the latest trends in problematic use, there is no wholesale figure for the total number of addicts. The only basis available for making such an estimate is to assume a proportion of *re-notified* to *new* addicts.

The University of Manchester, which manages the North West of England DMD, has estimated that the number of new clients reported in the DMD represents only two-thirds of the total number of individuals receiving treatment at any one time. If we can assume that this figure holds for the rest of England, a factor of 1.5 can be used to estimate from the RDMD figures the total number of individuals receiving treatment for their drug use in England and who are likely, by implication of the agency they are attending, to be receiving treatment – which in this case is drug dependency units (DDUs) and statutory drug services.

For the six month period ending March 1998, 15,735 new people were notified as starting treatment at DDUs and statutory drug agencies to the English RDMD. Using the factor of 1.5, it can be predicted that 23,602 people in England were in treatment during that period.

Table 3.2 | **Number of people starting and continuing treatment in England only**

Period	RDMD new notifications	Total treated using multiplier of 1.5
October 1998 to March 1999	15,735	23,602
April 1998 to September 1998	16,519	24,778
October 1997 to March 1998	14,136	21,204

Estimating the number of addicts in and not in treatment

While Table 3.2 provides an estimate of the number of addicts in treatment, it fails to cover those experiencing problems but not receiving treatment. Although it is almost impossible to count the number of people experiencing problems at any one time, there are ways of guessing.

Capture-recapture

A number of local studies have used what is called the capture-recapture method. Originally used to estimate the number of fish in a pool, this method simply calculates the number of recaptured or missed fish every time the net is cast, and applies this ratio to the whole population. In essence, two consecutive samples of the same population are taken. The first sample tags and releases all that are captured. The second then reveals the number of fish recaptured and those that are not (by way of the tags). This ratio can then be applied to the rest of the population. Therefore, if, on the second sampling, five out of 100 fish are tagged, then we can estimate that every time we cast the net, we catch only 5 per cent of the total fish population. From this we can estimate that in that pool, there are roughly 500 fish.

Using this method, several studies have estimated the number of problematic drug users in their area. In 1984, Hartnoll[21] collected data on the number of opiate users in North London who had attended a drug clinic and those admitted to hospital for infectious diseases. Comparing the sources, they found that a fifth of the hospital sample had also attended the drug clinic. The researchers used this ratio to estimate that the total number of opiate users was five times the number who attended the drug clinic.

It is difficult to know whether a multiplier is valid today and for all drugs. Whatever the figure, however, the number of drug users in treatment greatly underestimates the number of people dependent on one substance or another. Using the early 1998 revised biannual figures from the RDMD (see Table 3.2 above), we can estimate the total number of addicts in England by applying this multiplier of five. Using this formula, we can predict that for the six months ending March 1998, there were roughly 118,010 (23,602 x 5) drug addicts in England.

It is important to consider the diversity of drug users included in this total figure. Some of them will continue to be addicted for the whole six months, while some will have stopped – possibly entering a problematic period and exiting it quickly within the six-month period. The figure, therefore, represents those addicted for the whole period as well as those not. At any one point in time, therefore, the estimated total figure will be much less, due to many people stopping or starting after or before that point. A more detailed estimation for any one point in time, therefore, must take into account different user characteristics and using patterns to understand who is likely to still be experiencing problems with use and who is likely to have stopped or not yet started.

Factors affecting this estimate are availability and accessibility of treatment services, and people's willingness to seek treatment. With increased effort being

3

3

made to encourage the uptake of services, the ratio is expected to fall.

Morbidity – drug-related illness
HIV
Information on the prevalence of HIV and AIDS among drug injectors in England and Wales is provided by the Communicable Disease Surveillance Centre of the Public Health Laboratory Service through its unlinked anonymous HIV prevalence monitoring programme. The programme gets its data from screening the saliva of injecting drug users attending specialist treatment and support agencies or genitourinary medicine clinics in England and Wales. The sampling is neither random nor comprehensive, and fails to screen those not attending participating clinics, failing to do a saliva test or failing to declare their injecting.

England and Wales
The figures for 1997[22] show that the presence of HIV infection among drug injectors attending specialist agencies was 3.9 per cent for men and 1.5 per cent for women in London, and 0.37 per cent for men and 0.41 per cent for women outside the capital. Across England and Wales, prevalence among injectors has steadily declined throughout the 1990s and there is currently little evidence of new drug-related HIV transmission. Prevalence among injecting drug users (IDUs) continues to be much lower than in other Western European countries of comparable size.

Scotland
Information from Scotland is provided by the Scottish Centre for Infection and Environmental Health (SCIEH). The figures are for all persons coming forward for a named test and who are tested in an NHS laboratory. Cases are referred for testing from a wide range of settings – GPs, GUM clinics, counselling clinics, prisons, drug clinics, hospital inpatients/outpatients, etc. Coverage is national (not sampled), as all positives tests are confirmed by one of the main reference labs in Edinburgh or Glasgow.

In 1997, 36 injecting drug users were reported as being HIV+ in Scotland (72 per cent of whom were male) and the following year 18 were reported (94 per cent being male). The cumulative total number of HIV+ drug injectors is 954.

Edinburgh and Dundee have been the sites of the only significant drug-related outbreaks of HIV infection in the UK. Since the high infection rates of the late 1980s, the number of HIV-infected IDUs is on the decline in Scotland. In 1991 there were 52 new cases, with 25 in 1998 (85 per cent male), giving a cumulative total of 1,210 for 1998. Unsurprisingly, most HIV-infected IDUs are in Lothian and Glasgow, together amounting to 68 per cent of the Scottish total.

Hepatitis

Hepatitis C

Figures for hepatitis C are gathered by the Unlinked Anonymous Prevalence Monitoring Programme. Unlike HIV, hepatitis C is equally high among IDUs in and outside London.

The general trend in England and Wales for hepatitis C is downward, from 24 per cent for men in 1996 in London to 23 per cent in 1997, and from 18 per cent to 14 per cent for women. Outside of London, 17 per cent of men and 20 per cent of women attending agencies in 1997 tested positive for hepatitis C, again a fall from the previous year. In Scotland however, the number of known hepatitis C cases among IDUs has been rising rapidly since the late 1980s, from six cases in 1989 to 811 cases in 1997. This trend needs to be monitored, particularly among vulnerable groups such as prisoners and IDUs.

Hepatitis B

Hepatitis B figures are based on laboratory isolates reported to SCIEH. There is very little in the way of epidemiological information collected, which means that the figures will most likely contain a number of duplicates. Like the HIV and hepatitis C registers, data is collected on a national level, with all NHS labs from all health boards reporting.

Figures for 1998 in Scotland show that 58 IDUs were known to be infected with hepatitis B. Although not a large number, this is the fourth annual increase since 1995 and is likely to increase over the next decade.

Mortality

Data for drug-related deaths is collected by the Office for National Statistics (ONS). Annual articles are produced in the ONS publication *Health Statistics Quarterly*[23] with summary tables containing data for the most recent year. The first of these was published in February 2000, containing data for 1993-1998.

The ONS database of drug-related deaths records all deaths in England and Wales for 1993-7 where the underlying cause of death was assigned one of the following codes according to the International Classification of Diseases (Ninth Revision) (ICD9):

292	Drug psychoses
304	Drug dependence
305.2-9	Non-dependent abuse of drugs
E850-E858	Accidental poisoning by drugs, medicaments and biologicals
E950.0-5	Suicide and self-inflicted poisoning by solid or liquid substances, drugs and medicaments

3

3

| E980.0-5 | Poisoning by solid or liquid substances, undetermined whether accidentally or purposely inflicted – drugs and medicaments |
| E962.0 | Assault by poisoning – drugs and medicaments. |

This data has been entered in such a way that deaths can be sorted, counted and analysed according to any substances which are mentioned on the death certificate. For each record the database also contains information collected at death registration – eg, age, sex marital status, place of death, occupation and place of usual residence (to postcode level). Deaths involving more than one drug or alcohol can also be identified.

In 1997, there were 73 solvent-related deaths.[24]

There are various problems associated with quantifying deaths from specific drugs. The coroner can note any drugs implicated in a death in the 'cause of death' section of the coroner's certificate of death. However, coroners do not always know or record this information, often recording only a general description such as 'drug overdose'. Many deaths involve a mixture of drugs, often taken in combination with alcohol, and there is usually no recorded indication of the relative quantities or which substance was likely to have caused death. It is, therefore, not possible to obtain precise figures on deaths caused by specific substances using data collected at death registration.

ONS estimates of the number of deaths due to specific drugs are therefore based on the number of deaths where the *underlying* cause of death was drug-related (ie, assigned one of the ICD9 codes above) and where the drug is mentioned on the coroner's certificate, regardless of whether it was the *primary* cause of death. The figures presented in the Table 3.3 should therefore be regarded as an estimate of the number of deaths associated with particular substances rather than the exact number directly due to these substances.

Note: As heroin breaks down in the body into morphine, the latter may be detected at post-mortem and recorded on the death certificate. Therefore, where heroin and/or morphine were mentioned on the death certificate, a combined figures is included.

Table 3.3 | **Number of deaths where selected substances were mentioned on the death certificate, including with other drugs and alcohol, England and Wales, 1993–1997.**

	1993*	1994	1995	1996	1997
Heroin	67 (14) (13)	127 (31) (26)	162 (33) (33)	241 (51) (62)	255 (47) (56)
Morphine	129 (48) (28)	176 (51) (40)	231 (68) (61)	281 (74) (72)	255 (78) (68)
Heroin/ morphine	187 (61) (39)	276 (78) (61)	355 (93) (83)	464 (113) (120)	445 (112) (109)
Methadone	230 (92) (49)	269 (110) (57)	310 (130) (58)	368 (141) (87)	421 (152) (102)
Cocaine	12 (4) (0)	24 (12) (4)	19 (10) (2)	18 (8) (5)	38 (21) (5)
MDMA	8 (3) (2)	27 (12) (3)	10 (3) (1)	16 (8) (4)	11 (8) (1)
MDEA	2 (0) (0)	0 (0) (0)	1 (0) (0)	3 (2) (0)	1 (1) (0)
MDA	3 (0) (0)	1 (1) (0)	0 (0) (0)	0 (0) (0)	1 (1) (1)
Other amphetamine	24 (16) (4)	23 (17) (3)	38 (21) (5)	33 (20) (8)	40 (23) (2)
LSD	0 (0) (0)	1 (1) (0)	1 (1) (0)	0 (0) (0)	1 (1) (1)
Cannabis	14 (12) (6)	18 (16) (3)	17 (16) (5)	11 (11) (7)	13 (12) (2)
Temazepam	173 (115) (66)	163 (95) (50)	138 (102) (43)	98 (67) (28)	104 (78) (39)
Diazepam	55 (45) (29)	72 (64) (32)	76 (68) (26)	97 (91) (44)	122 (111) (56)
Nitrazepam	23 (14) (9)	18 (12) (4)	17 (10) (2)	11 (8) (3)	14 (7) (2)
Barbiturates	44 (11) (10)	46 (10) (4)	46 (8) (0)	30 (10) (7)	20 (6) (1)
Paracetamol compounds	463 (147) (96)	468 (146) (100)	526 (161) (106)	480 (145) (106)	561 (151) (129)
Paracetamol	322 (128) (56)	284 (106) (49)	323 (126) (44)	284 (112) (55)	345 (118) (71)
Co-proxamol	135 (19) (36)	187 (40) (49)	189 (30) (54)	188 (30) (44)	214 (30) (57)

(1st) Where another drug(s) was mentioned on the death certificate

(2nd) Where alcohol use was also mentioned on the death certificate

* Provisional

Note: Some deaths may be counted more than once in the table above. For example, if heroin and cannabis are recorded on the death certificate, the death will be recorded once under heroin and once under cannabis.

3

3

Drug-related road accidents

In 1997 the Department for the Environment, Transport and the Regions (DETR) began a three-year study (the first for 10 years) into the incidence of drugs in road accidents. The latest data, although preliminary, reveal that 6 per cent of road accident fatalities had traces of medicinal drugs in their system, while 16 per cent had illicit drugs and 34 per cent alcohol above the legal limit. These figures reveal the presence of a drug but do not reveal whether the person was under the influence at the time of the accident – eg, cannabis can remain in the body for up to four weeks after use. The figures do reveal, however, a high and increasing incidence of drug use and driving, particularly among the under 30s, which is likely to be associated with road accidents.

Following increased concern about drug-related road incidents, the UK Anti-Drugs Co-ordinator commissioned the Advisory Council on the Misuse of Drugs (ACMD) to report on the number of drug-related deaths, including road incidents. The ACMD report was published in spring 2000.

1. Hayes G and Baker O (1998) *Drug Prevalence in the UK: Update* 1998, London: ISDD.

2. The 1994 BCS for example shows that Greater London had the highest prevalence rates for younger and older respondents, and for different recall periods.

3. Bridgwood A et al (1998) *All Change? The Health Education Monitoring Survey one year on: The* 1997 *follow up to a survey of adults aged* 16-74 *in England carried out by Social Survey Division of ONS on behalf of the Health Education Authority*, London, HEA & ONS.

4. Tasker T et al (1999) *Drug Use in England: Results of the 1996 National Drugs Campaign Survey*, London: HEA.

5. A quota sample selects people on the convenience to the researcher, such as grabbing people at a shopping centre or putting an ad in the paper and then asking them questions. A random sample, such as the BCS, selects names randomly from a database, seeks them out and then questions them. Random samples tend therefore to be more representative of the population than quota samples, which often tend to pick people with certain characteristics, such as 'go shopping on a Monday afternoon' or 'reads ads in daily papers'.

6. Although the BCS claims to measure prevalence for Britain, one of its major drawbacks is that it fails to include Scotland and Northern Ireland. Despite this, some figures for the 1996 Scottish Crime Survey are available, but figures for Scotland, Wales and England as of yet cannot be combined to produce a complete UK picture. Where statistics for Scotland are available and differ greatly from the BCS they will be mentioned alongside the BCS figures but will not be compared directly due to methodological differences.

7. Boyle M and Morgan S (1997) *Drugs in Northern Ireland – Some recent survey findings*, Northern Ireland Office research findings, Belfast: Northern Ireland Office.

8. Balding J (1998) *Young People in* 1997, Exeter: Schools Health Education Unit.

9. Balding J (2000) *Young People and Illegal Drugs into* 2000, Exeter: Schools Health Education Unit.

10. Haselden L, Angle H & Hickman M (1999) *Young People and Health: The health behaviour in school-aged children*, London: HEA.

11. A Classification of Residential Neighbourhoods (ACORN) grades households according

demographic, employment and housing features of the immediate locality. The BCS uses six categories: thriving, expanding, rising, settling, aspiring, and striving.

12. CACI (1993) *ACORN User Guide*, London: CACI.

13. Parker H, Bury C & Egginton R (1998) *New Heroin Outbreaks Amongst Young People in England and Wales*, Police Research Group, Paper 92, London: Home Office.

14. Release (1997) *Release Dance & Drugs Survey: An insight into the culture*, London: Release.

15. Branigan P, Kuper H & Wellings K (1997) *The Evaluation of the London Dance Safety Campaign*, London: London School of Hygiene & Tropical Medicine.

16. Flemen K (1997) *Smoke and Whispers: Drug and youth homelessness in central London*, London: The Hungerford Drug Project.

17. Bennett T (1998) *Drugs and Crime: The results of research on drug testing and interviewing arrestees*, London: Home Office.

18. Singleton N, Farrell M & Meltzer, H (1999) *Substance Misuse Among Prisoners in England and Wales*, London: Office for National Statistics.

19. Bennett T (1998) *Drugs and Crime: The results of research on drug testing and interviewing arrestees*, Home Office Research Study 183, London: Home Office.

20. Audit Commission (1996) *Misspent Youth: Young people and crime*, London: Audit Commission.

21. Hartnoll R, Daviaud E, Lewis R & Mitcheson, M (1999) *Drug Problems: Assessing local needs. A Practical manual for assessing the nature and extent of problematic drug use in a community*, London: Drug Indicators Project.

22. Unlinked Anonymous Surveys Steering Group (1998) *Prevalence of HIV England and Wales in 1997: Annual Report of the Unlinked Anonymous Prevalence Monitoring Programme*, London: Department of Health.

23. Available from the Office for National Statistics or The Stationery Office outlets, or telephone 020 7533 5240.

24. "Drug-related deaths. Written answers." *Hansard*: 28 July 1998, col. 174.

3

4

how do drugs affect children & the family?

TEXT | **JANE MOUNTENEY** & **GARY HAYES**

YOUR | QUESTIONS | **ANSWERED**

How many pregnant drug users are there? | What are the effects of drugs on the

foetus? | What are the effects of withdrawal on the mother and child? | How do

drugs affect the family? | What support is available for mothers and children? | Are

there any laws which relate to parents and children? | What guidelines are there

which relate to parents and children?

4

How many pregnant drug users are there?

Female drug users

While reliable figures on the extent of drug taking are hard to obtain, it is clear that drug misuse has increased disproportionately among women. National figures suggest that for every three male drug users presenting to services, there is one female user.[1] However, it is assumed that this greatly underestimates the real figure. Considering that most woman conceal drug use and a high proportion of users do not come forward for treatment, this can be regarded as a significant underestimate. Explanations that have been offered for this are that:

- treatment services are less appropriate to women's needs
- social norms make it difficult for women to present.[2]

A number of studies have found that women feel more stigmatised for their drug use than men.[3] Female drug use conflicts with the traditional view of women as carers, mothers and wives. A common concern of women drug users presenting to services is that their children may be taken from them, and many services have tried to reduce this fear with positive policy statements.[4]

In the period 1 October 1997 to 31 March 1998, 9,183 females made initial contacts with drug agencies in the UK. The majority of these were in England (7,522), with 260 in Wales and 1,401 in Scotland. The 1998 British Crime Survey[5] suggests that over two-fifths (42 per cent) of women between the ages of 16-29 will try drugs.

Pregnant drug users

Over 30 per cent of registered addicts in the UK, and over 90 per cent of all females presenting to services, are women of childbearing age.[6] Hospital reports indicate an increase in babies born to mothers using a variety of drugs – in particular, opiates. A 1993 national survey of maternity units in England and Wales found that over 11 per cent of notified female drug users had given birth. There were estimated to be 568 deliveries to drug misusers over a 12-month period.[7,8]

What are the effects of drugs on the foetus?

The answer to a question such as "I took some x before I found out I was pregnant. Is it likely to hurt the baby?" is almost certainly "no". There are many factors affecting the level of damage a drug can do to the foetus. The main ones are:

- amount of drug taken
- over how long a period
- the physiology of the baby.

Evidence of drugs affecting the foetus is patchy and at times unreliable. There are a number of reasons for this:

Foetal damage studies often include retrospective and self-reporting drug assessments, extrapolation from animal studies, and the taking of inadequate case histories.

Clinicians and public health officials often play safe by simply stating what foetal damage has been reported after use of a drug, without estimating how frequently it happens.

It is difficult not to take a moral or alarmist stance on this area. Research from scientific press can also come under this influence, as a study by Koren et al[9] demonstrated, when adverse effects were reported more than their absence, despite the validity of their evidence.

Given these limitations, what follows is a review of the current state of knowledge about the possible effects of different drugs on the foetus.

General problems with drugs

For pregnant drug users in general, irrespective of the drug used, and especially where poor social conditions prevail, there is an increased risk of:

- low birth weight: caused by prematurity and intrauterine growth retardation
- perinatal mortality – death within the first week of birth (often caused by prematurity)
- congenital abnormalities, which for drug users are in the high–normal range of 2.7-3.2 per cent of all women who give birth. The greatest risk is in the first three months of gestation when the foetus is forming and the mother may be unaware she is pregnant. After the first three months, growth retardation may be a problem
- sudden infant death syndrome, also known as cot death.

Individual drugs

Tobacco

There is no evidence that the risk of congenital abnormalities is increased by smoking cigarettes, although heavy smoking has been associated with:

- low birth weight (ie, babies weighing less than 2.5 kilograms)
- reduced oxygen supply to the foetus due to reduced levels of oxygen in the mother's blood. One study showed that even if smoking is stopped for only 48 hours, there is an 8 per cent rise in available oxygen for the baby
- reduced blood flow because, as a stimulant, nicotine constricts the blood vessels
- increased incidence of cot deaths
- perinatal mortality, mainly associated with low birth weight, but some associations with tobacco.

Alcohol

There is a large body of evidence which suggests an association between alcohol and foetal harm. However, to quote the Department of Health's *Sensible Drinking* report, "A major problem in interpreting the human studies is the large number of confounding factors, including poor nutrition, licit and illicit drug intake and

4

4

smoking, all of which have known adverse effects on pregnancy".[10]
The same report concludes the following with regards to heavy drinking:
- Chronic drinking has the potential to induce the following effects:
  - abortion
  - foetal growth retardation
  - facial and other dysmorphologies
  - impaired postnatal physical and mental development.
- Most studies agree that two units of alcohol per day and above may be associated with reduced birth weight. However, there is no good evidence that one or two units per week have any diverse effect.
- Studies suggest that binge drinking can also produce the effects listed above. The recommendation is that women who are pregnant or likely to become pregnant, should keep their alcohol intake substantially below limits suggested for non-pregnant women – currently at 21 units a week.

Amphetamines

There is no good evidence of any link between amphetamine use and congenital abnormalities.

Benzodiazepines (tranquillisers, Valium, Librium, etc)

Studies have shown a link between benzodiazepine use in the first trimester of pregnancy and a mouth deformity known as cleft palate – all of the various benzodiazepines should be treated as having the potential to cause malformations. Breastfeeding can be a problem with cleft palate babies, who may have trouble sucking.

Caffeine

There is some limited evidence to suggest an association between caffeine consumption in excess of 300mg a day (approximately five cups of instant coffee or tea) and a small decrease in birth weight. Irregular foetal heart rate has been associated with very large daily amounts of caffeine intake late in pregnancy, but this returns to normal after caffeine intake is stopped.

Cannabis

A study in Canada,[11] which compared cannabis users to non-users, found there were no significant differences in rates of miscarriage, type of presentation at birth, frequency of obstetric complications, birth weight or physical birth defects, among even the heaviest users. There was some evidence of slightly shorter (about a week) gestation periods among the heavier smokers. Other studies that have shown adverse effects (eg, prematurity, low birth weight) for the babies of heavy cannabis users, have involved women whose drug taking, diet and general lifestyle have been more potentially detrimental than the effects found in the Canadian study.
The most recent review of cannabis by the World Health Organisation,[12] failed

to demonstrate any distinct problems for infants or children linked to parental use of cannabis during pregnancy.

Cocaine and crack

Possibly more than any other drug, heavy cocaine or crack use in pregnancy has been associated with harmful effects on the foetus, most seriously premature rupture of the membrane. Foetal growth is also retarded, due, it is thought, to the strong stimulatory effect on the circulation – ie, it restricts the supply of blood and oxygen to the foetus. However, as with most of the research on the adverse effects of drug use on the foetus, the studies suggesting such associations have been conducted with women from very poor socio-economic backgrounds where more general problems for babies are more likely to occur in any case. Also, many of the women in these studies had little or no antenatal care.

A study of social cocaine users[13] (ie, not dependent) who stopped when they realised they were pregnant, concluded that no adverse effects were experienced.

Ecstasy

There are no published case reports implicating use of ecstasy in foetal damage.

Heroin and other opiates

The main direct effect of opiate use in pregnancy appears to be low birth weight babies. There is also evidence of growth retardation with heroin use.[14] Other effects such as prematurity are at least in part associated with factors such as poor diet and ill health. Irregular use of heroin in pregnancy can cause foetal distress in labour and significant respiratory problems after delivery. See box "Neonatal Abstinence Syndrome", page 71 for the effects of withdrawal.

LSD

In the 1960s LSD was the subject of much press scaremongering. There is no evidence of foetal damage caused by LSD.

Solvents

Inhaled solvents reduce oxygen levels in body tissue and easily cross the placenta, so sniffing during pregnancy theoretically might reduce oxygen supply to the foetal brain, although there appear to be no cases on record. However, there is a study by Goodwin[15] which suggests an association between chronic daily paint sniffing (toluene) for several months and renal problems in the newborn.

What effect does withdrawal have on the mother and child?

Many drug-using women who find they are pregnant, will want to come off drugs, seeing the pregnancy as an opportunity for a change of lifestyle. Withdrawal from drugs can cause problems, mainly as a consequence of the physical trauma, and

4

4

success depends on the mother's ability to stay stable and healthy. The main effects and complications are briefly discussed below.

Stimulants

Substitute withdrawal or maintenance (see Chapter 8, for definitions) is not appropriate for stimulant drugs (amphetamine or cocaine) and is potentially harmful to the foetus.

Benzodiazepines

When benzodiazepines have been taken in ordinary therapeutic doses they should be withdrawn on an outpatient basis. The whole point of the withdrawal regime is to prevent fits. A one-week detoxification period is adequate on medical grounds, but on social grounds a longer period may be required if a woman cannot cope.

Heroin and other opiates

Traditionally, detoxification during pregnancy has been viewed as dangerous as it carries an unacceptable risk of spontaneous abortion or pre-term labour. However, detoxification mid-trimester is generally considered safe if a strict regime of reduction is followed. Therefore, methadone substitution or maintenance therapy tends to be advocated. A pregnant woman can choose in- or outpatient detoxification. Where the pregnant user does not have an overly unstable lifestyle and has support at home, outpatient detox can prove a more successful option , although it is less widely available. The advantages of outpatient detox are:

- methadone doses can be adjusted to prevent either intoxication of withdrawal symptoms
- the foetus can be monitored
- the availability and use of other drugs can be restricted
- other services such as counselling and exercise is more readily at hand
- stability can be restored to a normally chaotic life in some circumstances.

Breastfeeding

Most drugs do not pass into the breast milk in quantities which are sufficient to have any major effect on the newborn. With opiates, for example, the quantities ingested are so small that they will not prevent the onset of the neonatal opiate withdrawal syndrome. Breastfeeding is encouraged in mothers who are using drugs as long as the user is stable and the breastfeeding is not suddenly stopped. There is some variation among the benzodiazepines. Diazepam passes into the milk, and can cause sedation in the child. Chlordiazepine and nitrazepam also go into the breastmilk, but in quantities too small to have an effect.

Women who are HIV positive, or whose HIV status is unknown, are advised not to breastfeed. Studies show that if an HIV-positive mother breastfeeds her baby, there is twice the risk of passing on the infection, especially if the mother has only recently been infected.

Neonatal Abstinence Syndrome (NAS)

Overall, the likelihood and severity of withdrawal symptoms in the baby are broadly parallel to the level of drug use by the mother, with not all babies necessarily showing any symptoms. While the signs and symptoms are to some extent unspecific and symptomatic of many complications, they are characteristic and, in combination, recognisable to an experienced worker. Withdrawal symptoms are:

- Sleeplessness, restlessness/irritability, sneezing, sweating, abnormally rapid heart rate, tremors, vomiting, yawning, fever, fist-sucking, hyperflexia, diarrhoea, nasal stuffiness, respiratory depression and convulsion.
- A baby is likely to develop NAS if the mother has been regularly, or sometimes even intermittently, taking opiates, tranquillisers, barbiturates (or other sedative type drugs) during her pregnancy. In the case of long-acting drugs, such as benzodiazepines, withdrawal may be delayed for many days.
- Administering to the baby a controlled withdrawal regime using the dependent drug or a substitute can relieve unnecessary suffering and in a short space of time get the baby drug free.

HIV/AIDS and hepatitis

Various studies show the risk of mother-to-baby transmission of HIV ranges from 14 to 39 per cent. All infants born to HIV-positive mothers will have maternal HIV antibodies; however, this does not mean they will be necessarily infected.

Hepatitis B is common among injecting drug users. The transmission routes are the same for HIV, but the disease is even more infectious. Hepatitis B may be transmitted from mother to child, although prompt immunisation of babies born to known carriers has proved effective. Infection, if it occurs, will happen in the first three months of life.

Hepatitis C is also common among injecting drug users but far more dangerous than hepatitis B. Up to 50 per cent of all carriers develop serious liver disease.[16] Immunisation for hepatitis C is not possible and the only reliable test is a nonstandard (and therefore expensive) PCR (polymerase chain reaction) test.

How do drugs affect the family?
Children of drug-using parents

Recently in the UK there has been increasing concern about the effects of drug use on women of child-bearing age. The concern is twofold. On the one hand are the effects of drugs on the foetus and on the other, isolated incidents where children of drug-using parents have been neglected and consequently died.[17]

There is growing evidence of emotional, behavioural and learning problems experienced by many children of problem substance users. Klee identifies a num-

4

4

ber of potential impediments to a child's health and welfare, including poor bonding with mothers, poor parenting skills, uncontrolled drug use, and poor uptake of professional help.[18] However, several studies have found that children of substance-using parents are comparable to children of non-using parents from similar backgrounds. A 1996 study showed no difference between the health and development of children born to and reared by mothers who used opiates when pregnant and who remained on methadone, and a group of age- and socially-matched children.[19]

Drug use among young people

In this section we examine research into the possible reasons for drug use among young people. There are as many reasons for taking drugs as there are users. There is, however, a large body of research, again mostly from the USA, which looks at commonalities among drug users. Most of this research starts from the premise that drug use is a deviant behaviour and, therefore, the negative result of a number of antecedents, which in most cases it is not (see also Chapter 2). In effect, much of the research takes the medical view that drug use among young people is a disease. The data is largely useful for looking at problematic use or use which is excessive.

Risk and protective factors

The main points of the literature on these studies can be summarised using the terms – "risk" and "protective factors". These factors define traits, behaviours or situations, which, if found, are linked (usually causally) to negative or positive outcomes respectively – eg, addiction/poor health or low/non-problematic drug use. Examples of risk and protective factors are as follows:

Risk factors

- child abuse and maltreatment has been linked to later problematic substance use
- excessive parental drug use that has a direct influence on family life has been linked to later problem drug use in a child
- drug use at a very young age (under 14 years of age) is linked to later problematic drug use
- a child's access to their parents' drugs can result in use and, in particular, high risk overdose
- extreme economic deprivation has been shown to be a strong predictor of heavy drug use, although surveys in Britain[20] have shown that drug use is as common among young employed people living in private accommodation
- marginalisation such as school exclusion, sleeping rough or living in care is also linked to high levels of drug use.

Protective factors
- sources of support and influence such as partners, grandparents and on occasion support workers have a positive effect on children's well being
- religious affiliation, particularly as a family unit, is linked to lower substance use

Note that although drug use among young people is a minority activity, use among 16-25 year olds is common, with nearly half of some age groups having used a drug at least once.[21] Drug use is increasingly being seen as a normal activity that occurs chiefly because drugs are available, and drug use is seen as a desirable activity among the young.[22]

Where can parents and children get help?

There are types of support for parents and children. The main ones are listed here.

Drug rehabilitation and families

Since 1993, as a result of the NHS and Community Care Act (1990), social services departments have the responsibility for undertaking assessments of need for people misusing drugs and alcohol in their area and devising individual care plans. They also have fund-holding responsibilities for residential rehabilitation placements and a continued-care management role with these clients.

Treatment and services

In England there are 15 drug dependency units which work only with drug-using women. Most of these are in the south. There are also 15 women-only drug treatment services in England and Wales.

In addition, there are 146 treatment services that target women as well as men. Some of these work specifically with drug-using mothers and their children. Organisations such as the Aberlour Child Care Trust in Scotland, Marie Soper Project, Maya Project and Phoenix House Family Services all assist with parent and childcare skills as well as issues relating to drug use. Aberlour also helps children develop relevant strategies to deal with their vulnerability to drug misuse themselves.

Education and prevention

There are a number of drug education projects across the UK with activities targeted at young women. For example, Druglink in North Staffordshire runs a women-only project, as does the Hungerfield Drug Project in London.

Information services

DAWN (Drug and Alcohol Women's Network) is a national organisation working to advance education and training of those working in the drug and alcohol fields. It also provides information and produces policy guidance.

4

4

Family-specific legislation

There are a number of acts and laws that apply to women and children. The main ones are:

The Children Act 1989 (England and Wales)[23]

Section 17 of the Children Act 1989 enables the local authority to provide services and support to families where a child is considered to be in need. This may be used to provide services such as advice, counselling, home support or family centre placements to drug-using parents and their children. Local authorities are also encouraged to work in partnership with parents and are required to produce Children's Service Plans, which should take into account health and education for children and their families.

The local authority is under a duty to safeguard and promote the welfare of children and prevent their ill treatment and neglect. They are under a duty to make enquiries if they suspect a child is suffering or likely to suffer *significant harm*. The term significant harm is used to describe ill treatment or impairment of health or development that is sufficient to warrant public intervention.

If significant harm is suspected, authorities are likely to convene a child protection case conference to assess risk and decide whether the child should be placed on the child protection register. There are a range of options open to the local authority, depending on the particular case and level of concern. They range from family support (eg, helping the family or extended family to meet the child's needs) through to section 8 orders (where a child may be removed from the family, and the parent/carer allowed contact with the child only under certain conditions determined by the court). Most children with their names on the child protection register remain with their families, and courts are required to consider very carefully what action they should take in relation to children. A court is prohibited from making any order unless it is satisfied it will promote the child's welfare.

Children (Scotland) Act 1995

The Children (Scotland) Act establishes the duty of the local authority to safeguard and protect the welfare of children within their area who are in need, and to promote the upbringing of such children by their families through the provision of an appropriate range and level of services.

Section 19 of the Act requires local authorities to produce Children's Service Plans which should take into account health and education provision for children and their families. Scotland's Children Act (1997) provides guidelines on the support and protection of children and their families, noting especially that children whose parents use drugs must be included in Children's Service Plans. The Act also introduced three new court orders to protect children considered to be at high risk of significant harm.

What practice and policy guidelines are there?

Over the last few years there have been a number of new policy documents published that give guidance to those who work with, and are responsible for, children. Many of these focus on children who may be at particular risk, including those with drug-using parents.

Social Inclusion: Pupil support (1999)

This circular, published by the Department for Education and Employment (DfEE), offers guidance on dealing with drug-related incidents in schools, in relation to exclusion.

The Right Response: Managing and making policy for drug-related incidents in schools (1999)[24]

These guidelines, published by SCODA, aim to reduce the number of young people excluded from school because of drug-related incidents. They outline ways of identifying vulnerable groups, such as children with drug-using parents, and suggest that early intervention is appropriate.

The Right Approach: Quality standards in drug education (1999)[25]

Published by SCODA at the same time as *The Right Response*, this publication follows on from DfEE guidance on the responsibility of schools and the youth service to deliver high-quality drug education to all young people. It is a tool to help schools deliver their programmes of drug education.

Protecting Young People: Good practice in drug education in schools and the youth service (1998)[26]

This provides guidance to head teachers, the youth service and local education authorities on planning, evaluating and delivering drug education to young people.

Drug Using Parents: Policy guidelines for inter-agency working (1997)[27]

Published by the Local Government Drugs Forum and SCODA, these guidelines highlight good practice for statutory and non-statutory agencies, demonstrating the importance of joint work to provide effective services for drug-using parents and their children.

1. Department of Health (1999) *Statistical Bulletin: Statistics from the Regional Drug Misuse Databases for six months ending March 1998*, London: DoH.
2. Hunter G & Judd A (1998) 'Women injecting drug users in London: the extent and nature of their contact with drug and health services', *Drug and Alcohol Review*, 17 pp 267-76.
3. For example, Barnard M A (1993) 'Needles sharing in context: patterns of sharing among men and women injectors and HIV risks', *Addiction 88*, pp 805-12.
4. Thom B (1986) 'Sex differences in help-seeking for alcohol problems: the barriers to help-seeking', *British Journal of Addiction*, 81, p 777-88.

4

4

5. Ramsay M and Partridge S (1999) *Drug Misuse Declared in 1998: Results from the British Crime Survey*, London: Home Office.

6. Standing Conference on Drug Abuse/Local Government Drugs Forum (1997) *Drug Using Parents: Policy guidelines for inter-agency working*, London: Local Government Association.

7. Morrison C (1995) 'Maternity services for drug misusers in England & Wales', *Health Trends*, 27 (1), p 15-17.

8. Siney C (ed) (1995) *The Pregnant Drug Addict*, Books for Midwives Press.

9. Koren G et al (1989) 'Bias against the null hypothesis: the reproductive hazards of cocaine', *Lancet*, 2 (8677) p 1440-42.

10. Department of Health (1995) *Sensible Drinking: The report of an inter-departmental working group*, London: HMSO

11. Fried P (1986) 'Marijuana and human pregnancy', in Chasnoff I J (ed) *Drug Use in Pregnancy: Mother and child*, Norwell, MA: MTP Press.

12. World Health Organisation (1997) *Cannabis: A health perspective and research agenda*, Report by Programme in Substance Abuse, WHO.

13. Graham K et al (1989) 'Pregnancy outcome following first trimester exposure to cocaine in social users in Toronto', *Veterinary and Human Toxicology*, (2) p 143-48.

14. Thornton L et al (1990) 'Narcotic addiction: the expectant mother and her baby', *Irish Medical Journal*, 83(4) p 139-42.

15. Goodwin T M (1988) 'Toluene abuse and renal tubular acidosis in pregnancy', *Journal of Obstetrics and Gynaecology* 71 (5) p 715-18.

16. Carey P (1995) 'HIV, pregnancy and the drug user', in Siney C, *The Pregnant Drug Addict*, London: Midwives Press.

17. Mounteney J (1998) *Children of Drug-Using Parents*, Highlight No. 163, London: National Children's Bureau.

18. Klee H et al (1998) *Illicit Drug Use, Pregnancy and Early Motherhood*, and *Drug Using Parents and their Children: Risk & protective factors*, Manchester Metropolitan University.

19. Burns E C et al (1996) 'The health and development of children whose mothers are on methadone maintenance', *Child Abuse Review*, 5: p 113-122.

20. Ramsay M & Partridge S (1999) *Drug Misuse Declared in 1998: Results from the British Crime Survey*, London: Home Office.

21. *Ibid.*

22. South N (ed) (1999) *Drugs: Cultures, control and everyday life*, London: Sage.

23. HMSO, *Children Act*, 1989.

24. Standing Conference on Drug Abuse (1999) *The Right Response: Managing and making policy for drug-related incidents in schools*, London: SCODA.

25. Standing Conference on Drug Abuse (1999) *The Right Approach: Quality standards in drug education*, London: SCODA.

26. Department for Education and Employment (1998) *Protecting Young People: Good practice in drug education in schools and the youth service*, London: DfEE.

27. Standing Conference on Drug Abuse/Local Government Drugs Forum (1997) *op cit.*

5a

drug use
and criminal
behaviour

TEXT | **TREVOR BENNETT**

YOUR | QUESTIONS | **ANSWERED**

What is the link between drugs and crime?

What is the statistical connection between drugs and crime? | What is the causal

connection between drugs and crime? | What research has been done in this area?

Original text from *The International Handbook of Addictive Behaviour* edited by Ilana Bell Glass, Routledge 1991, updated by Gary Hayes, DrugScope, 2000.

5a

It is widely believed that there is an association between drug use and criminal behaviour. This belief is based on the results of a substantial body of academic research, which has shown that drug use and criminal behaviour are related. This belief is also based on popular wisdom as revealed in the stereotype of the drug-crazed addict who will stop at nothing to obtain drugs or money for drugs. However, the wealth of evidence supporting a drugs–crime connection belies a poverty of knowledge in our understanding of this association.

The problem can best be explained by making a distinction between a 'statistical connection' between drug use and crime and a 'causal connection'. The former concerns whether drug use and criminal behaviour are found together - either in the same place or in the same individual. The latter concerns whether drug use and criminal behaviour are related to one another in any kind of meaningful or causal way.

There is a great deal of evidence on the statistical connection which has lead to some (but not full) agreement that there is a relationship between drug use and crime. There is much less evidence available on the causal connection. Until the nature of the relationship between drug use and criminal behaviour is understood, the evidence of a statistical association is of little importance and has limited policy implications.

The statistical connection

Research on the statistical association between drug use and crime uses three main methods of investigation. The first is referred to here as studies of 'national and regional trends', which examine the relationship between broad movements in drug use and broad movements in crime. The second is referred to as studies of 'drug-using criminals', which examine drug use among samples of criminals. The third is referred to as studies of 'criminal drug users' which examine criminal behaviour among addicts and other drug users. The words 'drug' and 'drug use' are used in this chapter to refer mainly to heroin and other opioid drugs.

National and regional trends

The relationship between crime and drug use was investigated by the 'ecological school' of Chicago sociologists during the 1930s, who argued that criminal behaviour and other social problems (including drug use) tended to be concentrated in certain areas of the city. The general findings of these studies supported their theories and showed that high rates of addiction were associated with high rates of crime and delinquency. Later studies conducted in New York City in the 1950s confirmed these early findings showing that drug use was most frequently found in areas of the city which had high crime rates.

Link of drug cost to crime

A common method of investigating the drugs–crime connection using aggregated data is to examine the relationship between the price of heroin and crime. Studies of this kind are based on a number of assumptions about the demand for heroin. First, they assume that the demand for heroin is fairly inelastic and will be unaffected by price. Second, they assume that the higher the cost of heroin the greater the amount of money needed by the pool of addicts to purchase the drug.

According to this research the relationship between heroin use and criminal behaviour can be observed by monitoring what happens during a price rise in heroin. If a rise in the price of heroin is not associated with a rise in criminal behaviour it would be assumed that addicts financed their drug use through legitimate means and that there was no evidence of a drugs–crime connection. Research which has used this technique has tended to show that there is a correlation between the price of heroin and rates of 'income-generating' crimes.

Ask an expert

Another technique of assessing the relationship between drug use and crime is to ask experts for their opinions. The findings of these studies are sometimes referred to as informed guesses or best estimates. The most common method used is to mail a questionnaire to a large number of professionals or experts working in the field of crime or drugs (senior police officers or hospital consultants) and to ask them what percentage of criminal behaviour they believe is drug-related. The findings of this research are remarkably similar to those obtained by more rigorous methods. Professionals tend to believe that between one-third and one-half of property crimes are drug-related.

Drug-defined crime

The total number of persons in the UK found guilty, cautioned or dealt with by compounding for offences against the Misuse of Drugs Act in 1998 was 127,700, over four times the number dealt with in 1988. Ninety per cent of these offences are possession charges (as opposed to supply, production or cultivation) and the vast majority are related to the possession of cannabis. However, there was an increase of 77 per cent (to 14,780) in the number of heroin offenders in just one year from 1997 to 1998. The vast majority of these drug offenders were young (average age 25) and male (90 per cent).

Drug-using criminals

Studies of drug use among criminals are usually based on samples of prisoners or samples of arrestees. Levels of drug use among prisoners prior to coming into prison are very high, particularly among male remand prisoners. A study by the ONS (Office of National Statistics) revealed that half of the male remand prisoners showed some signs of problematic drug use – eg, 40 per cent showed severe symptoms of dependence. Female remand prisoners were no less likely to show such symptoms, at 54 per cent (47 per cent assessed as severely dependent). Sentenced prisoners were slightly less likely to shows such signs, with 43 per cent

5a

5a

for men and 42 per cent for women showing moderate to severe signs of dependence (Singleton et al, 1999).

Other studies that aim to determine the proportion of drug users among criminals focus on arrestees. The usual research method is to interview or to conduct urine tests on a consecutive sample of individuals arrested by the police. In the UK, the NEW-ADAM project (New England and Wales Arrestee Drug Abuse Monitoring) tested arrestees in five locations across England. The study showed high levels of recent drug consumption: up to 61 per cent of the sample had taken at least one illegal drug. High proportions of arrestees tested positive for expensive drugs such as heroin/opiates (18 per cent) and cocaine/crack (Bennett, 1998).

Criminal drug users

Another group of studies provide evidence on the drugs–crime connection by drawing on samples of known addicts and determining by various means their involvement in criminal behaviour.

The most common method of this group of studies is to determine the proportion of particular samples of addicts who have been convicted for at least one criminal offence. The aim of this type of research is to arrive at an estimate of prevalence of offending – in other words, the percentage of the population of addicts who have at least one criminal conviction. The bulk of this research shows that the majority of regular opioid users receive at least one criminal conviction in their lifetime. Studies which compare the prevalence of conviction among opioid users and the prevalence of conviction among the general population show that opioid users are much more likely to be convicted of a criminal offence.

Another method is to determine the proportion of drug users who admit recent offending based on self-reports. These studies show, not surprisingly, that almost all addicts interviewed admit that they have committed some kind of drug offence (eg, possession or supply) during a recent period prior to the interview. More surprisingly, these studies show that between one-third and two-thirds of addicts admit to some kind of property offence – eg, shoplifting, theft, burglary. One US study conducted from a store front in East and Central Harlem found that 40 per cent of the street opioid users admitted committing a burglary within the last 28 days and 60 per cent admitted committing at least one act of shoplifting (Johnson et al, 1985).

The timing of the onset of drug use and the onset of criminal behaviour is important as it tells us not only about the relationship between drug use and crime but also something about the potential causal ordering of the two events. The usual method is to compare official records of first criminal conviction with either official records concerning the onset of drug use or self-reported first drug use. These studies show that a high proportion of drug users had a criminal conviction prior to drug use. A study of arrest referral schemes in England, for example, showed that drug use for most of the arrestees became a problem in their early twenties, while the average age of first criminal convictions was 17 years

(Edmunds et al, 1999).

Some studies look at the association between periods on and off drug use, and periods on and off criminal behaviour. One method is to look at the arrest rate of opioid users both when they are using drugs regularly and during periods of abstention. The National Treatment Outcomes Study (NTORS), which follows over 750 drug users in the UK through different treatments, found that reductions in regular heroin use, particularly heavy use, are strongly associated with reductions in crime (Gossop et al, 1999). Heavy users of heroin, for example, were 11 times less likely to commit crime if they stopped using heroin than those that had not stopped using.

The relationship between treatment of drug addicts and criminal behaviour is important from the point of view of treatment policy. It is hoped that addicts in treatment will not only abstain from drug taking during or following completion of the programme but will also abstain from criminal behaviour. Studies of this kind sometimes compare prescription groups with non-prescription groups in terms of reported criminal behaviour. The results of these studies show either that the prescription groups have lower criminal behaviour scores or that there is no difference between the two groups.

Another method is to compare the criminal behaviour of users in treatment with those not in treatment or to compare the criminal behaviour of users prior to treatment with the rates for the same individuals after treatment. NTORS, although it does not follow through after treatment and does not have a control group, does demonstrate the efficacy of treatment in reducing crime. The number of crimes among 753 of its clients was reduced to one-third of the intake levels after one year of treatment. This trend was found regardless of treatment type, including prescription groups.

Similarly, the study of arrest referral schemes found that referral to treatment helped reduce drug use levels and involvement in crime (Edmunds et al 1999).

It is interesting to speculate on whether drug users who retire or 'mature out' of addiction also retire from crime. There are no studies to my knowledge which address this issue. Research of this kind would be useful in determining the long-term association between drug use and criminal behaviour and might provide some insights into the causal connection between the two variables.

The causal connection

Research on the nature of the relationship between drug use and crime has focused on three kinds of association: the first is referred to here as 'drug use directly causes crime'; the second is referred to as 'drug use indirectly causes crime'; and the third is referred to as 'drug use and crime are interconnected'.

Drug use directly causes crime

There are relatively few writers who argue that drug use directly causes crime. This explanation is more common in the alcohol and crime literature, which argues

5a

that alcohol use can cause disinhibition, which can cause the release of anti-social tendencies.

Pharmacological explanations are rare in the drugs and crime literature. It has been argued that opioid use can lead to a destruction of the character of the user, which might lead to forms of behaviour that might otherwise have been considered unacceptable by the user. It has also been argued that any kind of depressant drug can lead to the same kind of disinhibition experienced under the influence of alcohol. However, there are few convincing explanations of the way in which opioid use leads directly to the motivation to commit property crimes.

Drug use indirectly causes crime

There are many more explanations of the relationship, based on the idea that drug use indirectly causes crime. The main explanation of this connection is referred to as the 'economic necessity' argument.

The economic necessity argument is that addicts are forced to commit crimes to support their drug-taking habits. It is argued that regular heroin users have to spend large sums of money (often quoted at between £50 and £100 a day) to pay for drugs on the black market. As many of these users are not in full-time or well-paid employment they must be funding their habits by illegal means.

Proponents of the economic necessity argument provide evidence for their view by pointing to the disparity between estimates of addicts' incomes and the costs of financing an opioid habit. The results of this research are generally impressive in their accounting skills and tend to show marked disparities between estimated costs and estimated incomes.

The findings of some of the research already mentioned is also used to support the economic necessity argument. The research shows that addicts who receive opioids on prescription tend to report lower offending rates than those not on prescription. It also shows that addicts commit fewer offences during periods of abstinence than during periods of drug use. It is believed that these findings show that when addicts no longer need to purchase drugs on the black market they no longer need to commit property crimes.

Other research provides competing evidence. One North American study showed that addicts have a number of economic options open to them apart from theft. Some income can be raised by selling drugs to other addicts. Addicts might raise funds from state benefits, from contributions from family and friends, and from begging and hustling.

Research conducted in this country shows that some addicts do continue to commit offences after receiving a prescription (Bennett and Wright, 1986). Some of the addicts interviewed admitted that their reasons for offending were unrelated to financing their addiction. Inciardi (1981) has argued that the 'enslavement theory' (ie, that users are forced into a life of crime in order to support their habits) is too simplistic. He points out that many addicts are involved in crime before becoming addicted and many addicts continue offending while in receipt of free drugs or while in receipt of an income from legitimate employment.

Drug use and crime are interconnected

This argument is based on the proposition that drug taking immerses the drug taker into a deviant world on the borderline of legal and illegal activity. In order to become an addict it is necessary to have access to drugs, which for most users must be through dealers and other contacts on the borderline of the criminal world. It has been argued that some prior contact with criminality is a necessary condition of drug use for many addicts.

What is not clear from studies into treatment, drugs and crime is the causation. Studies in general health treatments have repeatedly shown that participation alone in any course of treatment is beneficial to an individual's condition. It is not clear, therefore, from NTORS or the arrest referral schemes whether the reduction in drug use causes a reduction in crime, or whether the simple offer of support facilitates this. By entering treatment, the individual may, for many reasons, be less inclined to get involved in crime.

The relationship between crime and drugs is complex. When they occur together they are usually both components of a chaotic or problematic lifestyle. As Edmunds et al (1999) show, although 64 per cent of the arrestees started their drug use before committing crime, only 12 per cent were involved in problematic use before committing crime. This indicates that criminal activity and problematic use tend to occur together. Moreover, some studies have shown that no matter which type of drug is used, be it heroin or alcohol, the heavier the use, the more inclined an individual is to be involved in crime (Hammersley and Morrison, undated).

Criminality and addiction might also be interconnected because certain psychological or sociological conditions produce a propensity towards general deviance (rather than criminality or drug use) and that this general deviant disposition might lead to a wide range of rule-breaking behaviours. This again may be why many drug users have criminal convictions before they begin drug use.

Conclusions

The results of this body of research show that there is evidence of a statistical relationship between drug use and criminal behaviour. It is perhaps too much to say at this stage that the evidence is overwhelming as the research providing this evidence is largely a hotchpotch of mainly small-scale studies with varying research designs.

The results of this body of research are less informative about the nature of the relationship (assuming that there is one). There is some evidence for the view that drug use causes a financial problem for some users which can only be resolved by criminal pursuits. There is also some evidence that drug users commit crimes for reasons unrelated to their addiction, and that drug taking is just one part of a lifestyle which involves criminal activity.

It is possible that drug use may lead to criminal behaviour among those who

5a

5a

would not have otherwise committed an offence during their lifetime. It is more likely, however, that individuals who become involved in excessive or problematic drugtaking are the same individuals who become involved in criminal behaviour. At this stage the most realistic conclusion seems to be that problematic drug use exacerbates criminal behaviour rather than creates criminals.

Notes

Bennett T H & Wright R (1986) 'The impact of prescribing on the crimes of opioid users', *British Journal of Addiction* 81: 265-73.

Bennett T H (1998) *Drug Testing Arrestees*, Home Office Research and Statistics Directorate, Research Findings No. 70, London: Home Office.

Edmunds M, Hough M, Turnbill P J & May (1999) *Doing Justice to Treatment: Referring offenders to drug services*, Drugs Prevention Advisory Service Paper 2, London: DPAS.

Gossop M, Marsden J, Stewart D & Rolfe A (2000) 'Reductions in acquisitive crime and drug use after treatment of addiction problems: one year follow-up outcomes', *Drug and Alcohol Dependence* 58: 165-72.

Hammersley R & Morrison V, 'Crime amongst heroin, alcohol and cannabis users', Paper submitted to Medicine and Law, Glasgow: University of Strathclyde, undated.

Inciardi J A (1981) *The Drugs/Crime Connection*, Beverly Hills, CA: Sage.

Johnson B D, Goldstein P J, Preble E, Schmeidler J, Lipton D S, Sprung B & Miller T (1985) *Taking Care of Business: The economics of crime by heroin abusers*, Lexington: Lexington Books.

Singleton N, Farrel M & Meltzer H (1999) *Substance Misuse among Prisoners in England and Wales*, London: Office of National Statistics.

5b

what are the costs associated with problem drug use

TEXT | **MARK EDMUNDS, TIGGEY MAY, IAN HEARNDEN** & **MICHAEL HOUGH**

from Edmunds M, May T, Hearnden I & Hough M (1998)
Arrest Referral: Emerging lessons from research, London: Drug Prevention Initiative

5b

Introduction

For the 97 per cent or so of illicit drug users who have not (or not yet) encountered any serious problems associated with drug use, there is no convincing evidence of causal links between drug use and acquisitive crime. Certainly people may commit various forms of property crime, and use the proceeds to buy drugs. However, they will also use this money to buy alcohol, clothes, CDs, etc. One might perhaps point the finger at a consumerist life style as a causal factor behind the offending[1] but there is no reason to single out any particular item on which money is spent as the cause of the offending.

For problematic users, by contrast, the evidence is overwhelming of clear but complex links between drug misuse and crime. A growing number of studies have documented beyond doubt that problem users are now spending very large sums on drugs, and that few are able to support their use through entirely legal means.

Figure 1 shows estimates from various studies of the weekly spend of problem drug users.

Where possible, we have presented the mid-point value (the median) rather than the average (the mean). In our own work, we have found that averages tend to be skewed by a very small number of very heavy spenders who report weekly spends in excess of £1,500 per week. The table suggests that figures set out in the Green Paper *Tackling Drugs Together*[2] were rather conservative. An average spend

Figure 5b.1 | **Weekly spends of problem users**

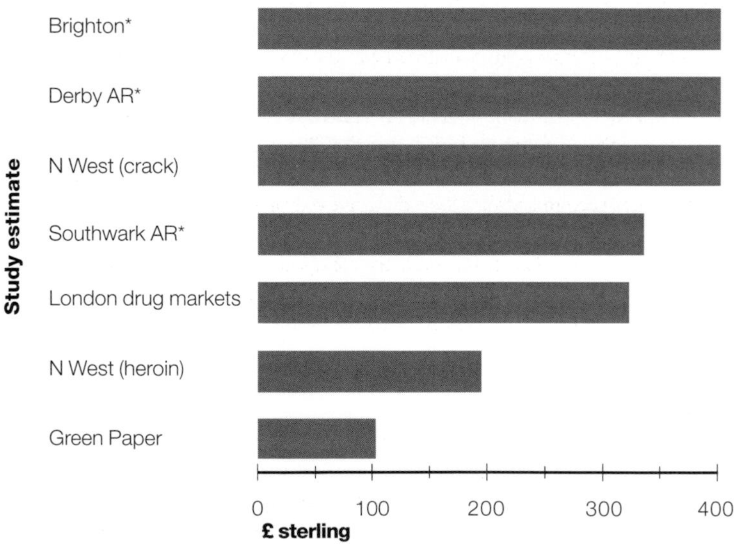

Sources: Edmunds et al;[3] Parker and Bottomley.[4]
*Estimates for these sites are medians, not means.

across the country of at least £200 per week among problem drug users may be more realistic.[5] If this is so, and if the national estimate of 130,000 problem drug users is tenable, it implies a weekly aggregate drug spend of £26m, or an annual spend of around £1.3b. If the population is closer to 200,000, the annual spend could exceed £2bn.

According to findings from our follow-up surveys[6] and to data we collected from police records, users raise money in a variety of ways, including theft, fraud, dealing, sex work, and the use of legitimate income such as benefits and earnings. Shoplifting, dealing and burglary are probably the most widespread methods used by problem users to raise money, with fraud being significant, and robbery rare. Many of those we have interviewed report dealing, at least intermittently, to raise cash, although only a minority raised their money primarily through dealing.[7] Following the methodology set out in the Green Paper *Tackling Drugs Together*, one can make estimates of the costs of this drug use to crime victims. Assuming that between a half and two-thirds of the £1.3bn is raised through acquisitive crime, some £650-£850 million has to be generated in this way. The costs to victims are much higher than this, because stolen goods are fenced at less than their market value. A factor of three was used in the estimates made in the Green Paper of costs to victims; this would yield a figure of around £2-£2.5bn. Whether users do manage to sell stolen goods for as much as a third of their market value is questionable; the fraction could be much lower, and the total costs to victims could thus be much higher. If a factor of five is nearer the mark than three, the total would be around £3-£4bn. Most of these costs are, of course, borne by organisations rather than individuals, and very often passed on to consumers. We have made no attempt to assess the non-financial costs to victims, which can obviously be considerable.

The complexity of the causal links needs stressing. As will be seen in Chapter 5, the majority of those whom we interviewed had long criminal histories, with an average of 21 previous convictions. Of the sample, 92 per cent had been arrested long before they recognised that their drug use was problematic. Whilst we cannot offer definitive evidence, it makes sense to conceptualise the causal links as dynamic or interactive. Criminal and drug-using careers often develop in parallel; stated simply, acquisitive crime provides people with enough surplus cash to develop a drug habit, and the drug habit locks them into acquisitive crime.[8]

Costs to public services
In addition to costs to victims, there are costs to public services, which are straightforward, if hard to measure. They include the costs to the health service of dealing with problem use and related ill-health, the costs to social security systems in providing unemployment or sickness benefit and housing benefit, and the costs to the criminal justice system in responding to drug-related crime. These costs are real, in that they create a demand on a finite public purse, and preclude other spending possibilities.

5b

5b

Costs to health and social services are hard to estimate. Expenditure on specialist drug services by health authorities and social services departments is probably in the region of £100m[9] (substantially in excess of the £41.3m nationally allocated for England by the Department of Health in 1997/98). Figures for generic health care are an unknown, but could be very high indeed. For example, a quarter of our sample of 128 had overdosed at least once in the month before contact with criminal justice drugs worker; 39 per cent recognised that their use had become problematic because of physical health problems. Problem users present the health service with a wide range of emergency and non-emergency demands. Then there are the costs of viral infection – notably HIV/AIDS and hepatitis. HIV/AIDS will impose high costs for a relatively small number of patients. Costs arising from the treatment of hepatitis B and C are likely to be substantially higher in the long term, given the greater prevalence – but it remains to be seen precisely how burdensome hepatitis C turns out to be.[10] We have no basis on which to estimate generic social services costs (eg in providing care facilities for the children of problem users), except to say that these are significant.

The vast majority of problem users are unemployed and claiming benefit; Regional Drug Misuse Databases suggest a figure of around 80 per cent. The majority will be claiming unemployment or sickness benefit, and many will be claiming housing benefit. If one assumes an average weekly benefit payment of £100 for 90 per cent of 130,000 problem users, the weekly bill is £12m (or £600m a year). It is unrealistic to attribute all this expenditure to problematic drug use. Indeed, some people may have developed drug habits precisely because of the limited life opportunities open to them, including those for employment. Nevertheless, any interventions which enable a problem user to return to the workforce will yield a saving of some £5,000 per person per year.

Costs to the criminal justice system

Costs to the criminal justice system can be estimated either by apportioning expenditure to offenders who are problem users or by estimating how many offences result in formal legal action, and apportioning costs to these crimes. The first approach involves estimating the number of problem users who pass through the criminal justice system annually, expressing this estimate as a proportion of offenders proceeded against, and applying this proportion to total criminal justice costs. For example:

- 130,000 problem users
- assume that 100,000 of them are criminally involved
- assume that 50,000 are arrested and prosecuted annually
- these would represent 10 per cent of all offenders prosecuted for notifiable offences, thus accounting for around 10 per cent of the £11bn spent annually on the criminal justice system.

The resulting figure of just over £1bn per year (or £10,000 per criminally-involved user) would need trimming down to take account of the proportion of police resources spent on non-criminal matters. One might assume, for example, that only a third of policing costs are directly absorbed by crime. If policing costs account for 75 per cent of the criminal justice spend, this would reduce the figure to around £500m, or £5,000 per criminally involved user. It is also worth bearing in mind that at least 15 per cent of the prison population are drug dependent on admission, suggesting that around £200m of the prison budget is absorbed by this group.[11]

Whether a figure somewhere between £500m and £1bn is plausible can be assessed by following the second approach, and looking at the costs of the criminal process in specific cases. Examples of average costs, updated from figures published by the Home Office[12] to correct for inflation, are:

- recording a crime: £100
- a pre-sentence report: £200
- a month remanded in custody: £2,000
- a contested trial in the Crown Court: £12,000
- a guilty plea in a magistrates court: £220 +
- a six-month prison sentence (with three months served): £6,000
- a one-year probation order without conditions: £1,200
- average system cost per recorded burglary: £600.[13]

Most criminally-involved problem users raise money through shoplifting, other theft and fraud. Take the case of a shoplifter who gets caught and prosecuted twice a year.[14] Let us assume that in each case there is a guilty plea, with a probation order in the first case and a two-month prison sentence in the second. Costs might be as follows:

£200	police costs for initial response to the two crimes
£800	for police costs in preparing two cases for the Crown Prosecution Service (CPS)
£400	for CPS costs in prosecuting two uncontested cases
£400	magistrates' court costs in dealing with two uncontested cases
£400	for two pre-sentence reports
£1,200	for one 12-month probation order
£2,000	for a 2-month prison sentence
£5,400	**Total**

Some problem users may stay out of contact with the criminal justice system for long periods. On the other hand, some pass rapidly through time and time again, and others, though less frequently prosecuted, incur high costs. Take the case of a

5b

drug-dependent burglar who may commit over 50 burglaries a year to fund a habit. If 50 of them are reported to, and recorded by, the police, the costs of initial police response and recording will be £5,000. There will be rather larger detective costs for cases that are investigated but not solved. The minority of cases resulting in detection and conviction will be very expensive: a single prosecution resulting in a year's prison sentence may involve a combined bill from the police, Crown Prosecution Service, Crown Court and prison services in excess of £15,000. The two approaches (see above) to criminal justice costs yield convergent estimates, which suggest that a total figure between £500m and £1bn is of the right order of magnitude.

Estimates for three research sites

Table 5b.1 applies the same methods and assumptions that we have used for national estimates, to yield local estimates in three research sites. We have slightly uplifted the average weekly spend, however, given that levels of expenditure in our three sites is higher than reported in other studies. The table poses the obvious questions whether the absolute level of investment in health care and criminal justice is right, and if the balance of expenditure between services is sensible.

Table 5b.1 | **Costs associated with problem drug use**

	Southwark	**Brighton**	**Derby**
Best guess at number of problem users	2,000	1,800	1,000
Average weekly spend	£250	£250	£250
Total weekly spend	£500,000	£450,000	£250,000
Total annual spend	£26m	£23m	£13m
Between 1/2 and 3/4 through raised acquisitive crime	£13m-£17m	£11m-£15m	£6m-£9m
Cost to victims (3 x cash raised through acquisitive crime)	£39m-£51m	£33m-£45m	£18m-£27m
Cost to criminal justice system £2,000-£5,000 per user	£4m-£10m	£3.6m-£9m	£2m–£5m
Expenditure on specific drug services (estimates)	£2m	£1 .5m	£1m

1. Parker H, Aldridge J and Measham F (1998) *Illegal Leisure: The normalisation of adolescent recreational drug use*, London: Routledge.

2. Home Office (1995) *Tackling Drugs Together: A consultation document on a strategy for England 1995-1998*, London: HMSO.

3. Edmunds M, May T, Hough M, Hearnden I and Van Rosenboom R (1997) *Get It While You Can: An evaluation*, A Report to Sussex Association for the Rehabilitation of Offenders, Sussex: SARO.

4. Parker H and Bottomley T (1996) *Crack Cocaine and Drugs-crime Careers*, Research Findings No. 34, London: Home Office.

5. This sort of expenditure could easily be incurred with a relatively light habit. For example, someone using 2.5 grams of heroin a week at a price of £80 a gram would hit this target; someone paying £50 a gram could afford 4 grams, or just over a half a gram a day. Our respondents included people who were spending almost £2,000 a week on a mix of heroin and crack.

6. Edmunds M, May T, Hearnden I & Hough M (1998) *Arrest Referral: Emerging lessons from research*, London: Drugs Prevention Initiative.

7. Assuming that the market would not allow someone to skim more than 15 or 20 per cent profit from street level dealing, a maximum of one in five users could finance their use exclusively through dealing.

8. Similarly sex work may facilitate regular drug purchase, and dependency may lock people into sex work with the added complication that drug use may make sex work more palatable.

9. Extrapolated from expenditure in three large health authorities – East Sussex, Brighton and Hove; Lambeth, Southwark and Lewisham; and Leicestershire.

10. Some 70 per cent of problem users are estimated to have hepatitis C (Strang J and Farrell M (1996) *Hepatitis Drugs Work*, London: ISDD) If only a small proportion develop severe liver problems, treatment costs will still be very significant. The likely costs of Interferon/combination treatment could in time be very high.

11. Extrapolating from estimates made in the late 1980s by Maden A, Swinton M, and Gunn J (1991) 'Drug dependence in prisoners', *British Medical Journal*, 302(6781), p 880.

12. Home Office (1992) *The Costs of the Criminal Justice System*, London: Home Office.

13. This figure represents the total system costs of dealing with all recorded burglaries, averaged across the total number of recorded burglaries.

14. The 60 users we interviewed when evaluating the Brighton Get It While You Can arrest referral scheme had an average of 1.6 convictions per year.

5b

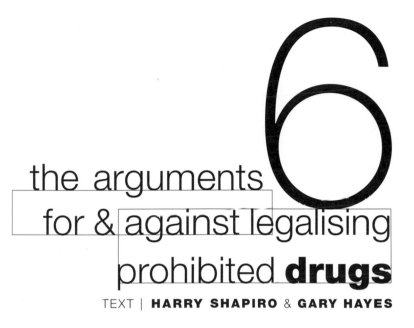

6

the arguments for & against legalising prohibited **drugs**

TEXT | **HARRY SHAPIRO** & **GARY HAYES**

YOUR | QUESTIONS | **ANSWERED**

What is the recent history of the debate? |

What are the key points in the debate?| What would be the impact

of legalisation? | What harm do the current laws cause? | How would

legalisation work? | Does cannabis lead to the use of other drugs?

The drugs legalisation debate raises all of the main issues around drug use: why people use them, why some think they shouldn't, freedom of choice, public health, and the role of law and order. This chapter looks at the legalisation debate and discusses the arguments on both sides of the fence. Most of the debate has centred around cannabis, which is discussed in detail here, but can be applied to all drugs.

The beginnings of the recent debate

Since the 1960s, there has been controversy over the prohibition of the non-medical use of cannabis, kept alive by a succession of campaigns aimed at reforming the law. Reforms proposed by successive pressure groups have been either the complete legalisation of cannabis smoking and the availability of a legal supply or the decriminalisation of cannabis whereby possession would not be a criminal offence, but perhaps akin to being given a parking ticket.

Support for reform has come from many quarters, including from within government. In 1968 the Advisory Committee on Drug Dependence recommended a limit of two years imprisonment for cannabis offences with no imprisonment simply for possession. These recommendations – contained in what became known as the Wootton Report – were rejected by the government of the day, with Home Secretary James Callaghan claiming that the committee had been unduly influenced by the pot lobby. Renamed the Advisory Council on the Misuse of Drugs, it made similar recommendations in both 1979 and 1982, which were similarly rejected.

During the 1990s, on the back of renewed interest about drugs among young people, the cannabis reform lobby sprang to life in various guises, ranging from the Green Party and the UK Cannabis Alliance making full use of the Internet to promote their views, to supportive editorials in the broadsheets and in particular the pro-reform campaign of the *Independent on Sunday*.

Some judges and serving senior policemen have expressed concerns about the viability of the existing laws, and the rapid growth of cautioning for simple possession of cannabis (and even other drugs) has been regarded as de facto admission that because of the large numbers of people who regularly flout the cannabis laws, it is wasteful of resources to push them through the judicial system.

Apparently frustrated by the government's refusal to enter into the debate in any meaningful way, the Police Foundation announced a three-year study into the workings of the Misuse of Drugs Act, while in 1998 the House of Lords decided to launch its own investigation into the medical evidence about cannabis.

Supporters for existing legislation, such as Parents Against Drugs, have repeatedly made reference to the health risks associated with its use and to the theory that cannabis acts as a gateway drug to the use of other more dangerous drugs such as cocaine and heroin. They are supported in this view by successive governments, none of whom have shown the slightest intention of relaxing controls on cannabis.

Sticking to convention

International solidarity is often cited by government officials as one of the main reasons for maintaining the current legislation against drugs. The UK is one of the 109 major industrialised countries which signed the 1961 UN Single Convention on Narcotic Drugs. As a signatory, the UK is obliged to make possession and other drug-related activities that involve a named set of drugs a punishable offence. Because of this, it is often thought that in order for any relaxation of the current legislation to take place the UK would have to opt out of the convention.

As other countries such as the Netherlands have made clear, there is a large degree of flexibility in the interpretation of the law, particularly around possession. Some consider possession as relating only to the act of trafficking, and not for personal use – ie, an individual found with a small amount of cannabis for personal use will not be considered as legally in possession of the drug. Other countries have deemed fines or censure as punishment enough for possession.

With this flexibility in interpretation, several countries have applied the convention in ways that best suit their approach to drug use. Only where there are 'serious offences' committed need a nation seek imprisonment. Countries that have relaxed their laws include Italy, Portugal and Spain.

What are the key points in the debate?

There are many discussions around drug legislation. How far do we relax the laws? What is the impact of each level of relaxation? Should we restrict legal drugs even more? Who should pay for the health consequences if more drugs are used? And so on...

On a generic level, the legalisation arguments can be broken down into four elements:

- civil liberties versus the duty of the state
- the consequences of drugs being made legal and therefore more available
- whether harm is caused by enforcing prohibition
- how a legalised regime would be managed.

Civil liberties
Freedom to use

Civil liberties have always been an issue in the debate; that is, the degree to which the state is justified in interfering in the private life of the citizen thereby restricting freedom of choice. The principle of personal choice is applied to a wide range of private activities and why not drug use? These concerns were sharply highlighted by the serious rioting in London, Bristol and Liverpool in the early 1980s. A major catalyst for public disorder were allegations that the police were misusing their wide powers to investigate drug offences to harass black youngsters on the streets.

6

6

Duty to protect

On the other hand, it is argued that if by using drugs an individual is causing significant harm to themselves or others, the state can rightfully seek to counteract that harm. In its duty to protect its citizens, the state has taken many steps in restricting what it sees as high risk behaviour. For example those travelling in cars are required by law to wear a seat belt, and those travelling on motorcycles must wear a motorcycle helmet. In legislating against drug use, the government is seen to be discouraging intoxication and therefore preventing potentially harmful behaviour which may not be of benefit to society as a whole.

Health impact

The issue about cannabis and health (as with other drugs) has probably been the central theme of the whole debate. A succession of national and international reports dating back to the last century have tried but failed to indict the moderate use of cannabis, although questions have remained about the long-term consequences of smoking a drug with mind altering properties.

The latest international review of cannabis was conducted by the World Health Organization (WHO) and published in 1998. Controversially, the WHO took the decision not to publish details of a review which showed that in many respects, users of tobacco and alcohol were running the same, and in some cases more, risks to their health than smokers of cannabis.

What happens elsewhere may not be applicable here in the UK. It is very difficult to predict what will happen in drug cultures from one country to another. For example, ecstasy has made a much bigger impact in the UK than in the USA, while PCP (Angel Dust) has been widespread in the States but virtually unknown here. Some argue that if we legalised and then had to re-impose a ban, more people would have been introduced to the drug during the period of licit supply, and would almost certainly carry on using it. Therefore, we would be worse off than before.

Others feel that by making cannabis illegal and talking about it in the same health terms as heroin and cocaine, we undermine the credibility of drug education in the eyes of young people. Education, it is argued, should focus more on the harmful aspects of drug use, instead of trying to convey a message that fails to address the most relevant issues.

On the other hand, many believe that any government legalising drugs would be sending out the message to society that intoxication is OK.

Whatever health harms might be caused by cannabis, the harms caused by the drug laws are regarded by some as worse. Those that believe this say we can only improve the situation by law reform. Evidence from the USA when some states decriminalised in the 1970s, and more recent evidence from Holland, shows that cannabis use does not rise dramatically with decriminalisation, leading many to conclude that such a move does not encourage more widespread use of other drugs.

The harm of current laws
While the purpose of drug laws is to prevent what the government sees as harmful behaviour, they are seen by some as harmful in themselves. They make users criminals, create strong and lucrative black markets and stigmatise those who need help the most – the addicts. Here are the main arguments for and against.

The arguments against prohibition
The worst aspect of prohibition is the way it hits the user. Many have been saddled with criminal records or even sent to prison just for possessing cannabis. Enforcement of drug laws causes tensions between police and otherwise law-abiding citizens. Users come into contact with criminal networks in order to buy drugs.

As well as potentially wrecking academic and career prospects, prohibition brings in its wake violence and corruption on a large scale, while making massive profits for organised crime. If the aim of prohibition is simply to reduce risks to health, it is a moot point that the means justifies the ends.

The arguments for prohibition
People who use illegal drugs knows the risks they are taking. People have to take responsibility for their own actions. Some reform options, like decriminalisation might make matters worse. It would do nothing to undermine the illicit market while encouraging more widespread use.

How would legalisation work?
Crucial to the debate on legalisation are the issues around the practicalities of one situation over another. On the one hand, making drugs legal and so more available will result in possibly more use and therefore more harmful side effects – at great cost to society as a whole. On the other hand, removing a black market and could raise drug-related revenues for the government. The main arguments for and against are presented here.

Arguments for making legalisation work
Legalisation would transfer huge revenues to the government by way of taxation as happens now with tobacco, while at the same time wiping out the illicit market and all the problems it creates. Regulating the markets will assure quality and remove the risk of receiving dodgy or even dangerous goods. Savings created by ending enforcement of the law are best spent on harm minimisation campaigns, on health, and on helping those who most need it, such as drug addicts.

Arguments against legalisation working
How realistic is it to imagine that drug syndicates would just give up trading in a commodity that currently nets them millions of pounds? Also, cannabis, unlike tobacco, will grow anywhere, so there is every chance that the illicit market would continue to supply cannabis as the licit product would be highly taxed. Even

6

today, otherwise legal products are counterfeited or adulterated and sold on the black market– legalising them will not eradicate this. The main questions around legalisation have not been fully addressed: What drugs? Who is going to have access to what? How do you regulate? Finally, the legal drugs cause the greatest harm and cost to society, by legalising other drugs, how do we know they will not cause equal harm?

Does one drug lead to another – the escalation theory

Because cannabis is the most common illegal drug, it is often the first illegal drug an individual will come into contact with. It is also the drug most commonly identified with legalisation. Cannabis is regarded, therefore, as the gateway to drug use and, of more concern, to problematic drug use – a reason often given for prohibiting its use. This section looks at the escalation theory – ie, moving from one drug to the next.

Although only a small proportion of those who try cannabis go on to use heroin, most people who use heroin will have previously used cannabis. This could be because cannabis actually leads (at least for some people) to heroin use. But there are alternative explanations.

For instance, it could be that heroin and cannabis use are both caused by something else in the individual's personality or background that the researchers have not taken into account. Also, the studies suggesting cannabis use might lead to heroin use have been done in Western societies at a time when cannabis is more freely available than heroin. This could mean people tend to use cannabis first simply because they come across it first.

Even if cannabis use did lead to heroin use, there would remain the crucial issue of exactly how this happened. The assumption is that if cannabis leads to heroin, then more cannabis use would result in more heroin use – an argument against legalising cannabis. But the reverse could be the case. For instance, it could be that cannabis use involves people in the buying of illegal drugs, making it more likely that they will meet with an offer of heroin, an offer some will accept. In this example, it would be the illegality of cannabis use rather than cannabis use itself that led most directly to heroin use. The implication is that some heroin use might be prevented by legalising cannabis, even if this meant more widespread cannabis use.

This example illustrates the fact that the mechanism of any link between cannabis and heroin may be as important as whether or not such a link exists in the first place.

The Netherlands is often cited as providing evidence that decriminalisation of the possession of small quantities of cannabis does not lead to the use of other drugs. A number of Dutch studies have suggested that decriminalisation actively distances cannabis users from the use of other drugs by removing cannabis retailing from the black market. The Dutch Ministry of Justice in particular has stated that a process of escalation does exists, but only where a single criminalised market exists. Drug prevalence figures comparing the Netherlands with other countries has shown not only that cannabis use is much lower than that of the UK (up to 70 per cent less according to a European Survey comparing international prevalence figures), but that cannabis users are less likely to have used other drugs such as cocaine, amphetamine and heroin than those in the UK and other countries including the USA.

All that can be said definitely is that:

- The use of other illegal drugs is generally preceded by cannabis use.
- Cannabis use does not necessarily (or even usually) lead to the use of other illicit drugs.

The following are some quotes from the current debate:

"If you import cannabis you get 25 years – is importation of cannabis four times as bad as rape?"

"There is a vast amount evidence which suggests cannabis is not a danger to life. It's certainly not the same kind of crime that rape is. And do the penalties we impose deter? The statistics tell us absolutely plainly that they do not. Deterrence has in my view absolutely no role at all."
Lord McCluskey at the Law Society of Scotland's 50th Anniversary conference, 1999.

"The truth is that most people I know have smoked at some time or other in their lives. They hold down jobs, bring up their families, run major companies, govern our country, and yet, after 30 years cannabis is still officially regarded as a dangerous drug."
Rosie Boycott, Editor, Independent on Sunday, 2000

"It now seems to be fashionable and politically correct to call for the decriminalisation of cannabis, but I would be very sorry if this... paved the way for a freer availability and a new drug culture"
David Alton, Liberal MP and vice-chair of the All Party Parliamentary Drugs Misuse Group.

"Crude decriminalisation will not work... Something more subtle is needed ... and is already in operation in Holland ... Soft drugs... are decriminalised through prosecution policy... hard drugs should not be legalised, but we should review the old British idea if making them available to addicts on prescription."
Guardian leader, 14 October 1993.

6

7

what are the UK's anti-drug strategies?

TEXT | **GARY HAYES**

YOUR | QUESTIONS | **ANSWERED**

What is the UK international approach to drugs? | What is the UK International

Strategy? | What are the UK international and frontier controls? | Who are the UK's

international partners? | What is the UK domestic approach to drugs? | What is the

UK drugs strategy? | What are the Scottish, Welsh and Northern Irish strategies? |

What are the UK domestic drug controls and laws?

7

Introduction

The following chapter begins by looking at the UK's international approach to drugs. This is followed by a look at the UK domestic approach, examining how this is owned by the four UK nations and how it is applied regionally and locally.

The UK international approach to drugs and its partners

The main elements in the UK's strategy for dealing with international drug matters are through bilateral representations and multilateral action. The UK with its unique position in the UN, European Union and Commonwealth seeks a coherent approach across the three organisations by way of its international drugs strategy, which draws together international and domestic agencies in tackling trafficking and demand.

Tackling drugs: the UK's international strategy

The UK's international drugs strategy sets out a strategic approach to the UK's international drugs effort. Overseen and monitored by a Co-ordinating Committee comprising interested Whitehall Departments and law enforcement agencies, the strategy has the following principal objectives:

- to reduce the flow of illicit drugs into the UK
- to promote and enhance effective international co-operation against all aspects of the illicit drugs trade.

The strategy states that the objectives can be achieved by a range of actions, and that effective UK mechanisms must be in place to achieve them. The actions are principally:

- direct interdiction of illicit drugs, from source of supply to entry into the UK
- disruption of trafficking organisations
- reducing the profitability of supply by action against money laundering
- control of precursor chemicals essential to the manufacture of illicit drugs
- reduction of production at source.

Through these actions, the government is aiming for a coherent and comprehensive strategy to tackle the problem from source of supply through to the point of consumption. It allows enforcement agencies to target criminals and their organisational structures (through arrests and disruption and dismantling of the organisations); their assets (through confiscation and anti-money laundering arrangements); the drugs themselves (through interdiction, eradication and alternative development programmes); and the precursor chemicals used in their manufacture (by effective international controls).

UK arrangements for dealing with drugs work outside the UK and its overall policy approach have developed in an evolutionary and ad hoc way. They include:

- law enforcement activity in liaison with foreign counterparts
- bilateral diplomatic activity, backed up by assistance to foreign governments
- multilateral engagement, mainly in the United Nations (UN), European Union (EU), Financial Action Task Force (FATF) and G7/8, but also in less formal groupings such as the Dublin Group which brings together EU and other donor countries to co-ordinate policies and international assistance.

The international and frontier controls

UK law enforcement overseas

Vital to the national and international anti-drugs operations is the role played by British drug liaison officers (DLOs) who work as part of the diplomatic staff at British missions. Over 50 DLOs are stationed in the principal drug-producing and transit countries – ie, those countries through which drugs regularly travel. Drawn from both Customs and police, the number of DLOs is increasing.

National Criminal Intelligence Service

The National Criminal Intelligence Service (NCIS), staffed by both police and Customs officers, takes a lead role in the gathering of intelligence about the activities of major drug syndicates. It is a multi-agency organisation. Created in 1992, NCIS is responsible for the collection, analysis, research and dissemination of intelligence relating to major criminals involved in serious crime, including the distribution and trafficking of drugs. NCIS has headquarters in London and five regional offices staffed by more than 500 police, Customs and civilian personnel.

NCIS does not conduct its own drugs operations. Individual police services, the National Crime Squad and Customs carry out the operational role in detection and prevention. The key objective of NCIS is to assist police and Customs by providing them with intelligence to help target major criminals and syndicates involved in the manufacture, distribution and trafficking of drugs.

One of the key roles of NCIS is risk assessment based on the intelligence it gathers. Where intelligence locates the bases of drug networks or strategic points for the transit of drugs targeted for Britain, NCIS can respond to the increased threat by careful targeting of extra resources.

The International Liaison Unit within NCIS is part of a division that has responsibility for the DLOs in Europe and for the UK's links with Europol and Interpol (the worldwide police organisation with its HQ in Lyon, France). An EU Convention giving Europol a legal basis to operate within Europe was ratified in 2000 and the Europol Drugs Unit is now working under a Ministerial Agreement. It is the aim that, with proper management, the work of Europol and Interpol is not duplicated.

HM Customs and Excise National Investigation Service

There are two principal aspects of Customs control for drugs. The first is preventive control at ports and airports and through coastal surveillance. The second is specialist investigations based on information and intelligence gathered from var-

7

ious sources at home and overseas, designed to anticipate and intercept consignments of drugs and arrest the organisers of smuggling attempts.

The National Investigation Service (NIS) was formed in April 1996 by an amalgamation of staff from the Investigation Division of Customs and the Collection Investigation Units. The amalgamation produced a national and international network of 1,700 investigators based in the UK and in British diplomatic missions (drugs liaison officers – see page 103).

The UK's international partners
In fulfilling its strategic aims, the UK works as a partner or member of the following leading international organisations:

United Nations
The UK supports and contributes to the United Nations International Drug Control Programme (UNDCP), formed in 1991 as the focal point in the UN for co-ordinating international assistance and action against drugs.

The UK is also an active member of the Dublin Group (part of the UNDCP), which brings together European Union and other donor countries to co-ordinate policies and assistance towards transit and producer countries. Several initiatives have been taken through local Dublin Groups to seek a greater commitment from governments in both transit and producer countries to tackle the illegal drug trade and introduce appropriate legislation.

The UK attaches particular importance to the 1988 UN Drugs Convention, which provides a comprehensive framework for international co-operation against drug trafficking. The UK ratified the Convention in June 1991, extending it to UK Dependent Territories.

Commission on Narcotic Drugs (CND)
CND is the body responsible for monitoring implementation of the UN drugs Conventions. It meets annually to review progress and discuss policies with a view to giving direction to member states and UN agencies, especially the UN International Drugs Control Programme.

Financial Action Task Force
The UK is an active (and founding) member of the Financial Action Task Force (FATF), established by the G7 in 1989 to develop international measures to prevent money laundering. The FATF has 40 recommendations, designed to promote best international practice in the fight against money laundering. The FATF's mandate up to and including 2003, which includes creating a global anti-money laundering network and expanding its membership was endorsed by G7 finance ministers in May 1998. UK money laundering experts regularly participate in FATF mutual evaluations of its members.

G8

The UK actively participates in the G8 Experts Group on Transnational Organised Crime (TOC) set up following the G7/8 Halifax Summit in 1995. The group's mandate was to identify gaps in international co-operation against TOC and propose practical action for improvement. A year later the group presented 40 recommendations to be implemented by states to help combat TOC.

Europe

The UK has played key roles in tackling drug problems across the European Union. The European Action Plan to Combat Drugs 2000 to 2004, first adopted by the Treaty of Rome in 1990, stresses the need for an integrated response based on four key elements:

- demand reduction
- supply reduction
- international co-operation and
- co-ordination at a national and union level.

The Treaty of Amsterdam (1997) introduces the objective of safety within "an area of freedom, security and justice". Article 116 in particular provides a legal basis for customs co-operation between member states. Such co-operation takes place through Europol and through the exchange of information by the Pompidou Group – the main forum for sharing of national expertise.

The European Monitoring Centre for Drugs and Drug Addiction (EMCDDA) was established in 1993 to provide the European Community and its member states with "objective, reliable and comparable information at European level concerning drugs and drug addiction and their consequences".

The EMCDDA co-ordinates a network of 15 national information centres for national focal points, one in each member state. Together with the EMCDDA, these centres make up the REITOX, the European Network on Drugs and Drug Addiction. Each national focal point, which for the UK is DrugScope, gathers data and publishes its national annual report on drugs and drug use, which includes government and non-statutory data and information. Contact the DrugScope library for details of the UK annual report or see the website: www.drugscope.org.uk

The UK domestic approach to drugs and its agents
UK co-ordination

At the UK level, the Ministerial Sub-Committee on Drug Misuse, chaired by the Minister for the Cabinet Office, co-ordinates the government's national policies for tackling drug misuse. It works across departments such as the Department of Health, the Home Office Action Against Drugs Unit and the Department for Education and Employment.

The UK Anti-Drugs Co-ordinator and his Deputy provide leadership and focus

7

7

in implementing the government's strategy and act as Special Advisers to the Minister for the Cabinet Office. In England they are responsible for the day-to-day implementation and monitoring of government policy and are supported by officials at the United Kingdom Anti-Drug Co-ordination Unit (UKADCU), which is a part of the Cabinet Office. Scotland, Northern Ireland and Wales have produced their own strategies, which reflect the key elements of *Tackling Drugs to Build a Better Britain*.¹j The UKADCU and its co-ordinators are advised by two important bodies – the Advisory Council on the Misuse of Drugs and the Drugs Prevention Board.

The Advisory Council on the Misuse of Drugs
The Advisory Council on the Misuse of Drugs (ACMD) was established under the Misuse of Drugs Act 1971. The ACMD currently has 32 members comprising academic experts and professional practitioners in the area of drug misuse. The bulk of ACMD's work is carried out by its committees and working groups. At present, its work includes prevention working groups on areas such as drug education in schools, volatile substance abuse, drug-related deaths, at-risk children, and drug misuse and the environment. There are also the Statistical and Research Committee and the Technical Committee, which advise on methods and areas for development. The ACMD reviews most areas of UK legislation, recommending changes where appropriate.

Drugs Prevention Board
One of the key functions of the Drugs Prevention Board is to consider the priorities for the prevention of use of illegal drugs, both in terms of activity and expendirue, taking account of the best contribution to be made by government and by those outside government, including trhe voluntary and business sectors.

The UK drugs strategy
A drugs strategy review was carried out after the appointment of the UK Anti-Drugs Co-ordinator in 1997, and in 1998 the government published *Tackling Drugs to Build a Better Britain: The government's 10-year strategy for tackling drug misuse.*

Regional co-ordination – drug action teams
Throughout the UK the implementation of the strategy is co-ordinated through multi-agency co-ordination at national and local levels. This primarily involves drug action teams (DATs) in Scotland and England, drug and alcohol action teams (DAATs) in Wales, and drug co-ordination teams (DCTs) in Northern Ireland. (Some DATs in Scotland are becoming substance action teams.) These teams lead and co-ordinate local efforts to tackle drug use (and they are hereafter referred to as DATs, unless otherwise applicable). The UKADCU issues an annual template for completion by the DATs. These are used to collect core information on local action and map the progress of each area in achieving set aims.

DATs compromise senior people from the local agencies concerned, advising and informing on optimal strategies for action in their local area. Each DAT can be supported by a number of drug reference groups (DRGs) in England or drug forums in Scotland. In Northern Ireland DCTs are structured such that they incorporate both elements of the DATs and DRGs. In Wales, local advisory teams (LATs) were set up. These advisory groups are made up of experts as well as community representatives, and are intended to help DATs draw up and implement the local strategy.

National support – DPAS
The Drugs Prevention Advisory Service (DPAS) provides advice and support across England. In operation since 1 April 1999 as part of the Home Office, the DPAS functions at national, regional and local level. It is organised in nine teams around government regional offices, with headquarters in London. The DPAS has an annual budget of £6 million, of which roughly £400,000 covers research.

The DPAS supports DATs in delivering the government's anti-drugs strategy, in particular aims 1 and 2 relating to helping young people resist drug misuse and protecting communities from drug-related anti-social and criminal behaviour. It is responsible for the management of the DAT Development Fund (currently £5 million), which is intended to support the effective running of DATs. The DPAS also aims to advance the cause of drugs prevention and expand the evidence base.

Strategy support for Scotland, Wales and Northern Ireland is discussed later in this chapter.

Tackling Drugs to Build a Better Britain
The strategy sets the government the task of examining: what works in tackling drugs, how to improve information structures, and how to track progress. It has six underlying principles: integration, evidence, joint action, consistency of action, effective communication and accountability. The strategy is founded on a vision of creating "a healthy and confident society, increasingly free from the harm caused by the misuse of drugs". To this end, there are four key aims against which the government has set itself key performance targets followed by shorter term measures. The four aims relate to: young people, communities, treatment and availability.

All strategic drugs activity operates under the umbrella of these four aims and ministers are bound by a Public Service Agreement to achieve them.

1. Young people
- **Government objective:** to "help young people resist drug misuse in order to achieve their full potential in society".
- **Key Performance Target:** to "reduce the proportion of people under 25 reporting use of illegal drugs in the last month and previous year substantially, and to reduce the proportion of young people using the drugs which cause the greatest harm – heroin and cocaine – by 50 per cent by 2008, and by 25 per cent by

7

7

2005".

- **Education:** The government has set itself the targets of having in place, by 2002, integrated, sustained and comprehensive programmes involving life-skills approaches in all schools, the youth service, further education, the community, and with parents, based on evidence of good practice.

The government has also set itself the task of reducing exclusions from schools arising from drugs-related incidents. DATs and local education authorities are charged with introducing training for teachers and for introducing drugs education into the school curriculum by way of personal social and health education (PSHE).

Prevalence

Establishing baseline figures has been the focus of much of the government's work in the first two years of the strategy. A number of studies into the prevalence of drug use have been carried out by the Office for National Statistics and DrugScope. The British Crime Survey also serves this purpose (see Chapter 3). By 2002 the government has set itself the aim of delaying the age of first use of class A drugs by six months and reducing by 20 per cent the number of 11-16-year-olds who use Class A drugs.

To aid this, the Drugs Prevention Board was created to take forward joint national commissioning of effective prevention and education and develop a programme of action to reduce young people's use of Class A drugs, particularly heroin and cocaine.

2. Communities

- **Government objective:** to "protect our communities from drug-related anti-social and criminal behaviour".
- **Key Performance Targets:** to "reduce levels of repeat offending among drug misusing offenders by 50 per cent by 2008 and by 25 per cent by 2005".
- **Crime:** In an attempt to break the perceived link between problem drug use and crime, by 2002 the government aims to have all police services operate face-to-face arrest referral schemes covering all custody suites. They aim also to significantly expand probation and court referral schemes in line with evidence from the Drug Treatment and Testing Order pilots.
- **Prisons:** The government set out its approach to drug use in prisons in *Tackling Drugs in Prison: The Prison Service drug strategy*, May 1998.[2] Set out with the same four key objectives as the overall drugs strategy, it aims to provide through-care for prisoners and young offenders (see CARATS, page 110), improve treatment facilities and referrals where appropriate (see DTTOs, page 110), and control the supply and use of drugs in prisons (see below), among others.

Restricting supply into prisons

To this aim prison governors have been given the powers to ban any visitor found smuggling drugs into prisons or young offender institutions. Prisoners found to be involved in smuggling may face closed visits, regular targeted mandatory drug testing and disciplinary proceedings.

Mandatory Drug Testing (MDT)

In an attempt to control the use of drugs in prison, a system of mandatory drug testing (MDT) has been introduced. In 1996/7, approximately a quarter of drug tests on prisoners in England and Wales were positive,[3] clearly demonstrating that drugs are still easily available inside. Prisoners who test positive face disciplinary action face such as having days added to their sentence. They may also be offered help in the prison's drug support programmes.

3. Treatment

- **Government objective:** to "enable people with drug problems to overcome them and live healthy and crime-free lives".
- **Key Performance Targets:** to "increase the participation of problem drug mis-users, including prisoners, in drug treatment programmes which have a positive impact on health and crime by 100 per cent by 2008; and by 66 per cent by 2005".
- **Treatment services:** One of the key features of the strategy is to improve the quality and coverage of treatment services. They aim to do this in the following ways:

Standards

National Occupational Standards for specialist drug and alcohol workers are being set in place, as are national quality standards for treatment programmes.

Clinical guidelines

- Treatment guidance for doctors and drug workers who work with problematic drug users is provided under what is termed the 'clinical guidelines' (Department of Health, 1999). The guidelines offer a framework from which to provide good practice, as well as outlining minimum care requirements, responsibilities, and accountability. Among some of the requirements, doctors and drug workers:
- must provide care for both general health needs *and* drug-related problems, whether or not the patient is ready to withdraw from drugs
- should not be put under duress by colleagues or patients to provide treatment beyond [that] standard unless s/he wants to
- should not prescribe alone (medical practitioners)
- should only offer substitute medication without specialist generalist or specialist advice (see below) in exceptional circumstances
- must ensure that the patient receives the correct dose and that appropriate

7

7

efforts are taken to ensure that the drug is used appropriately and not diverted
onto the illegal market
● should supervise consumption for new prescriptions for a minimum of three
months.

The guidelines introduce the concept of levels of expertise in treating drug users.
Each level is required to meet certain standards of care, receive training and seek
specified support and partnership.

Legal accountability under the guidelines
Although the guidelines on clinical management of problem drug users[4] have no
defined legal position, they set a standard against which disciplinary investigation
can take place. Any doctor, NHS or private, who departs from the set guidelines
and what they call 'standards and quality of care', will be liable to judgement under
the new powers granted to the General Medical Council under the Medical
(Professional Performance) Act 1995.

Prescribing
Currently any doctor wishing to prescribe heroin, cocaine or Diconal has to be in
possession of a Home Office license. It has been proposed, as part of the consultation for the clinical guidelines, that this be extended to all controlled drugs,
including oral methadone. Concerns that this extension would inhibit doctors
from engaging many opiate users in treatment, has lead to the proposals being put
to consultation in late 1999. Any changes to the current system require an amend-
ment to the Misuse of Drugs Act. MPs will not be asked to consider new
legislation until the end of next year with no new scheme in place until early 2000.

Prisons
The government has set itself the task of increasing the number of treatment programmes in prison and improving the service. Thirty new prison-based rehab
programmes are being introduced and it is expected that 5,000 prisoners a year
will undertake treatment programmes. Two programmes are also operating in this
area:

CARATS
The prison service has commissioned detoxification centres and a basic drug
advice, counselling and referral service CARATS (Counselling, Assessment,
Referral, Advice and Throughcare Services). The introduction of CARATS seeks
to establish an annual caseload of 20,000, taking in and following through the
treatment of prisoners (and those on probation).

Drug Treatment and Testing Order
The Crime and Disorder Act 1998 creates the Drug Treatment and Testing Order.
The Order gives courts the power to, with an offender's consent, require her/him

to undergo treatment for drug misuse. Two aspects of this approach are the role of the court in reviewing the offender's progress on the order; and the mandatory drug testing component. The probation service is funded to purchase access to a wide range of treatment requirements of the order. The probation service also provides the link between the treatment provider and the court. In the case of a breach, sentencers will have several options, including continuing or amending the order with an option for imposing an additional penalty; or, in the case of wilful and persistent non-compliance, revoking it and re-sentencing for the original offence.

4. Availability
- **Government objective:** to "stifle the availability of illegal drugs on our streets".
- **Key Performance Targets:** to "reduce access to drugs among young people (under 25) significantly, and to reduce access to the drugs which cause the greatest harm, particularly heroin and cocaine, by 50 per cent by 2008 and 25 per cent by 2005".
- **Drug distribution:** To help understand the dynamics of the UK's drug markets, drug distribution models are being put in place to estimate more accurately flows into Europe and UK. Drug supplying into prisons is also to be investigated by implementing a model to assess the levels and routes of supply and drugs within prison. They also aim to reduce the rate of positive results from random Mandatory Drug Tests from 20 per cent in 1998/99 to 16 per cent in 2002.
- **Enforcement:** The strategy identifies heroin and cocaine as the most harmful to society and aims to increase the percentage of heroin and cocaine seized as a proportion of overall availability.
- **Asset seizure:** Another key aim of the strategy is to increase by one third the amount of assets identified from drug traffickers and secured. In 1999, the Home Secretary outlined possibilities for the civil forfeiture of assets which are the proceeds of, or intended for use in, drug trafficking and other criminal conduct. No prior conviction in the criminal court would be necessary, as is normally the case at present. The forfeiture process would take place in civil proceedings, and it would be for the authorities to prove, on the balance of probabilities, that assets were the proceeds of, or intended for use in, drug trafficking or other criminal conduct.
- **Legislative controls:** There exists a number of legislative controls on the supply and the possession of drugs in the UK. See page 113, The UK domestic controls, for further information.
- **Scottish Drug Enforcement Agency:** The Scottish Drug Enforcement Agency co-ordinates the efforts of enforcement agencies to other drugs policies, such as education, treatment and demand reduction in general.

7

7

National variations on the UK strategy
Scottish strategy

May 1999 saw the publication of Scotland's drug strategy document *Tackling Drugs in Scotland: Action in partnership*.[5] This was endorsed by the Scottish Executive in May 2000 in the document *Tackling Drugs in Scotland: Protecting our Future*, which put forward the executive's Action Plan. The documents set out the same four key aims as indicated in the UK strategy and outlines Scotland's Objectives and Action Priorities, using similar key objectives to those outlined in the UK Anti-Drugs Co-ordinator's annual report.[6]

In the spirit of social inclusion, partnership, and evidence-based accountability, the Scottish strategy is underpinned by the following four key principles:

- Inclusion – tackle the causes of social exclusion
- Partnership – coordinated and collective work and partnerships across services
- Understanding – accurate research and information to underpin all work
- Accountability – set clear targets which can be properly evaluated.

Although the Key Objectives outlined in the Scottish strategy are referred to as the UK Key Objectives they do not have the same benchmarks, such as rates of crime or prevalence reduction over a set time period. Instead, the Scottish strategy concentrates on goals, such as providing drug education in all schools throughout the country and extending outreach work to young people.

National co-ordination
Overall responsibility for the strategy lies with the Scottish Executive. Charged with the monitoring and co-ordination of the strategy is the Scottish Advisory Committee on Drug Misuse (SACDM), which advises on:

- tackling progress on the strategy and ensuring its implementation
- overseeing the monitoring arrangements
- policy development
- oversight of the information and research requirements of the strategy
- adjustments required to the strategy in the light of experience.

SACDM is supported by two sub-committees and an effectiveness unit:
- the Operations Sub-Committee, which includes officials from the executive departments, members of the SACDM, and the Prevention and Effectiveness Unit (see below). This committee is charged with evaluating the work of the drug action teams and setting targets for the progress of the strategy
- the Research Sub-Committee, whose remit is to: review existing research; identify relevant existing material or material in preparation; identify priorities for new work, taking account of existing gaps in knowledge; and, oversee the preparation and publication of a drug misuse research programme to drive forward the implementation of the Scottish strategy. This committee comprises members of the SACDM, executive officials and independent researchers
- the Drug Misuse Prevention and Effectiveness Unit provides support in the

implementation of the prevention and effectiveness agenda of the Scottish drug strategy. Much of its work is consultative. The Unit's action plan will aim to determine and promote best practice. Its annual budget is £300,000.

Welsh strategy

Tackling Substance Misuse in Wales: A partnership Approach, launched in May 2000 has a broad substance misuse remit including alcohol, emphasizing the importance of partnership working. The draft strategy's focus on young people is extended to cover children and adults – with a remit to reduce prevalence and promote sensible drinking. A robust framework for monitoring progress in meeting the aims of the revised strategy is an important element of performance management.

There are two key national bodies which support the strategy. The Substance Misuse Advisory Panel provides advice at a national level in a similar way to the ACMD. The panel is made up of chairs of DAATs, with specialist panels on areas such as education, prison service, youth, etc. Each specialist panel is made up of relevant experts in the field. Offering direct advice and support in the implementation of the strategy is the Welsh Drugs and Alcohol Unit. Overall responsibility lies with the National Assembly, who submit an annual report to the UKADCU as part of their commitment to the overall UK strategy.

Northern Ireland strategy

Following a review of the current policy statement on drugs in Northern Ireland, a new drugs misuse strategy was published in August 1999. The *Drug Strategy for Northern Ireland*[8] is complementary to the strategies of the other UK nations, although the specific objectives seek to tackle the problems prevalent in Northern Ireland, where the use of heroin and other drugs is not as widespread as other parts of the UK. It has a five-year plan and introduces for the first time a Statement of Purpose – outlining roles and responsibilities of all contributing agencies and establishing overall objectives strategic framework. The Strategy's overall aim is 'to reduce the level of drug related harm in Northern Ireland'.

The Central Coordinating Group for Action Against Drugs (CCGAAD), chaired by the Minister of State for the Northern Ireland Office aims to encourage coordinated interagency approach to drugs problems in Northern Ireland. The Drugs Information and Research Strategy Implementation Team (DIRSIT), as a sub-group of CCGAAD, oversees the implementation of the strategy. As part of the Northern Ireland Drugs Campaign in 1996, four DCTs, similar to DATs in England and Scotland, were set up within each area health and social services board. This involved the development of action plans and working with local community groups.

The UK domestic controls

There are a number of UK legislative controls to restrict the supply and use of drugs in the UK. The following agencies are responsible for enforcing them.

7

7

National Crime Squad

The National Crime Squad (NCS) was set up in 1998 and is staffed by 1,450 police officers drawn from the 43 forces of England and Wales. In addition, some 380 support staff are also employed. The function of the NCS is to 'prevent and detect serious crime which is of relevance to more than one police area in England and Wales' (section 4(2) of the Police Act 1997).[9]

The NCS is divided into three geographical areas – eastern, northern and western – with national headquarters in London. The NCS is headed by a director general who holds the personal rank of chief constable.

The NCS strategy specifically addresses the Home Secretary's objective of suppressing the availability of controlled drugs in the United Kingdom by:

- reducing the unlawful manufacture and distribution of controlled drugs within the UK
- reducing the quantity of such drugs entering the UK unlawfully
- the arrest and prosecution of individuals leading to the dismantling or disruption of criminal enterprises engaged in serious and organised crime connection with illicit drug trafficking.[10]

In 1999, the NCS made 6,121 arrests for drug trafficking, disrupted and dismantled 214 criminal drug enterprises, and carried out 32 drug operations in close partnership with HM Customs and Excise.[11]

'Operation Bromley' is a good example of the multi-agency approach adopted by the NCS. This operation, led by the Hainault Branch Office and assisted by the National Criminal Intelligence Service (NCIS) Turkish Intelligence Unit and HM Customs and Excise, was set up to target the distribution of heroin by a large Turkish criminal organisation operation in London and the Home Counties. Five people were arrested for drug trafficking offences and 30 kilos of heroin seized, with a street value of £3-3.5 million.

National Criminal Intelligence Service

The NCIS was set up in April 1992 to focus intelligence-led enforcement effort against the nucleus of serious criminals whose activities posed a threat to UK interests. In 1997 the NCIS was placed on statutory footing. Its functions are to:

- gather, store and analyse information in order to provide criminal intelligence
- provide criminal intelligence to police officers in Great Britain, the Royal Ulster Constabulary, the NCS and other law enforcement agencies
- act in support of the Royal Ulster Constabulary (RUC), the NCS and other law enforcement agencies carrying out their criminal activities under section 2 of the Police Act 1997.

The NCIS Drugs Unit takes a lead role in the investigation of synthetic drug production, dealing with information about the diversion of chemicals worldwide. The Unit works with the chemical industry, the Home Office and police chemical liaison officers to gather intelligence on illicit drug production. Every year a number of illicit drug laboratories are uncovered and the manufacturers arrested as a result of the work undertaken by the Unit.[12]

Police drug squads
All police forces in Great Britain have drug squads or similar specialist units to deal with drug-related offending. For example, the Metropolitan Police Force (MPF) in London has a number of specialist units that focus their activity on drug trafficking criminal groups.

The Special Intelligence Section (part of the Criminal Intelligence Branch, New Scotland Yard) spends much of its time collating and disseminating intelligence on Jamaican and Turkish drug traffickers operating in and around London. The MPF Serious Crime Group (SCG) targets major drug traffickers. In July 2000, SCG officers seized 76 kilos of heroin with an estimated street value of more than £7.5 million.[13]

The drugs desk of the MPF Criminal Intelligence Branch (CIB) is responsible for providing strategic overviews on drug misuse and trafficking in London. Working with the Forensic Science Service Drugs Intelligence Unit, the CIB Drugs Desk has designated a database to monitor the price and purity of heroin and crack cocaine in London. The data is being used to help monitor the availability of these drugs.

The MPF Drugs Directorate is responsible for developing policy in London pertinent to the UK government's ten-year strategy for tackling drug misuse. The Directorate also works with the Association of Chief Police Officers (ACPO) Drugs Sub-Committee in helping to develop national policy and guidance documents on all matters relating to drug misuse and trafficking in England and Wales.

Scotland
The key drugs enforcement work in Scotland is carried out by members of dedicated drug squads and the criminal investigation departments of each of Scotland's eight police forces. The Scottish Crime Squad, consisting of over 100 specially-trained and equipped officers, concentrates on the more serious crimes – eg, high-level drug trafficking. In 1997-98, for example, it recovered £8.6 million worth of drugs.

Northern Ireland
Although all police squads deal with drug dealers and users, the RUC Drugs Squad is responsible for targeting resources for seizures and arrests in Northern Ireland.

Prisons
The Prison Service is responsible for preventing drugs being used and smuggled into prisons. All operational prison staff are trained in search techniques with the use of drug dogs, closed circuit television (CCTV) and mandatory drug testing among prisoners.

7

7

Controlling medicines

Many police forces have dedicated chemists inspection officers (CIOs). These specialist police officers carry out regular inspections of pharmacies to ensure they comply with regulations under the Misuse of Drugs Act 1971. CIOs have a particular responsibility for investigating offences committed by pharmacists and members of the medical profession.

The Medicines Control Agency (MCA) controls the sale of medicines by chemists and other retail outlets as defined by the Medicines Act 1968. The Medicines Control Agency defines a medicine as one which changes the body's physical or mental state. Under the Act, all such medicines may only be sold by a licensed chemist. Drugs such as poppers and GHB (see chapter 1) are controlled under the Act and so are monitored for sale by the MCA.

Legislation controlling supply
The Misuse of Drugs Act 1971

The Misuse of Drugs Act 1971 establishes the controlled status of drugs liable to be misused. The Act and its associated Misuse of Drugs Regulations render unlawful the importation and exportation, production, supply and possession of such drugs without authority. The Regulations also provide for the legal production and distribution of controlled drugs for pharmaceutical purposes and impose requirements in respect of prescription, record keeping and the destruction of drugs. The strictest controls are applied to those drugs with little or no acknowledged medical use.

The government aims to deter drug traffickers and dealers by providing high maximum penalties and by depriving them of the proceeds of their crimes. These deterrent effects have been strengthened by:

- The *Criminal Justice (International Cooperation) Act 1990*, which makes it an offence to manufacture certain substances which knowingly would be used in the unlawful production of a controlled drug.
- The *Criminal Justice Act 1993*, which substantially strengthened the existing powers for confiscating the proceeds of all types of crime including drug trafficking. The drugs provisions have recently been consolidated in the Drug Trafficking Act 1994, including the power to forfeit drug trafficking money which is being imported into or exported from the UK.

Medicines Act 1968

Governs the manufacture and supply of medicinal products, mainly drugs.

Customs and Excise Management Act 1979

Enforceable only by Customs & Excise, this Act allows for up to 14 years imprisonment for the import or export of Class A & B drugs.

Controlled Drugs (penalties) Act 1985

This Act increased the maximum sentence for trafficking in Class A drugs from 14 years to life imprisonment.

Intoxicating Substances (Supply) Act 1985

Controls sales and supply of solvents to those under 18 years of age in the UK except for Scotland. Scottish Common Law provides for a similar offence of "recklessly" selling solvents to children.

The Cigarette Lighter Refill (Safety) Regulations 1999

The Cigarette Lighter Refill (Safety) Regulations 1999 make it an offence to sell gas lighter refills containing butane to persons under 18 years of age. Retailers found guilty of not taking reasonable steps to avoid selling gas lighter refills to under 18s are liable to a maximum of six months imprisonment or a fine not exceeding £5,000. The provision came into effect on 1 October 1999.

Drug Trafficking Act 1994

Allows for the seizure of assets and income that cannot be shown not to have come from the proceeds of drug-related crime.

Legislation controlling possession

In terms of sentencing, the framework introduced by the Criminal Justice Act 1991 requires that sentences passed by the courts should be commensurate with the seriousness of the offence. Where a court considers that an offence is not so serious that only a custodial penalty is justified but is serious enough to merit a community sentence, the court must ensure that the order or orders it makes are the most suitable for the offender, and in doing so may take into account any information about the offender which is before it.

The Criminal Justice Act 1991 also empowers courts to order an additional requirement to be attached to a probation order stating that the offender should receive treatment for drug or alcohol dependency (see also drug treatment and testing orders, see pages 110 and 129). To do this the court must be satisfied:

- that the offender is dependent on drugs or alcohol
- that her/his dependency caused or contributed to the offence in respect of which the order is proposed to be made
- that her/his dependency is such as requires and may be susceptible to treatment.

'Dependency' is defined by the 1991 Criminal Justice Act as an individual having "a propensity towards the misuse of drugs or alcohol" and so can be interpreted widely. Drug treatment conditions could include a residential or non-residential period of contact with a drug agency. The treatment condition may be made for a shorter period of time than the full length of the probation order.

7

7

Road Traffic Act 1972
Includes legislation which makes it an offence to be in charge of a motor vehicle while unfit to drive through drink and drugs (including prescribed drugs and solvents).

1. HM Government (1998) *Tackling Drugs to Build a Better Britain: The government's 10-year strategy for tackling drug misuse*, London: The Stationery Office.

2. HM Prison Service (1998) *Tackling Drugs in Prison: The Prison Service drug strategy*, London: HMSO.

3. Wilson P (1997) 'Drugs in prison', in *Drug Users and the Criminal Justice System*, London: London Drug Policy Forum.

4. Department of Health (1999) *Drug Misuse and Dependence: Guidelines on clinical management*, London: The Stationery Office.

5. Scottish Office (1999) *Tackling Drugs in Scotland: Action in Partnership*, Edinburgh.

6. UK Anti-Drugs Co-ordinator (1999) *First Annual Report and National Plan: Tackling drugs to build a better Britain,* Cabinet Office/COI.

7. Welsh Office (2000) *Tackling Substance Misuse in Wales: A Partnership Approach*, Cardiff: National Assembly for Wales.

8. Northern Ireland Drugs Campaign (1999) *Drug Strategy for Northern Ireland*

9. National Crime Squad *Briefing Note 2000*

10. National Crime Squad *Strategic Plan 2000/2003*

11. National Crime Squad *Briefing Note 2000*

12. NCIS Annual Report 1997-1998.

13. *The Job*, Volume 33, Issue 833, London: MPS, 2000

where 8 to get help

TEXT | **GARY HAYES**

YOUR | QUESTIONS | **ANSWERED**

What types of treatment are there? | What types of drug services are available? |

What help is available for specific groups? | What is a good

service and what works?

There are a broad range of services and treatments available for people experiencing problems with drugs. This chapter outlines the main types of services available, the treatment options that can be found within them. It also provides information about how successful these treatments are for individual drug users and for society as a whole.

This chapter deals mainly with heroin dependency because in the UK heroin is the main illicit drug on which people become dependent and that treatment services are best equipped to deal with, although a section on specific groups describes other service provision.

The types of help available

Education, prevention and advice

A number of agencies and services offer advice on a range of issues, such as crisis intervention, legal advice, counselling, and drug information in the form of booklets, posters, help-lines, drop-in and peer education.

Peer education informs targeted, selected members of a particular group or social network and encourages them to pass on accurate information to others with similar characteristics.[1]

Needle and syringe exchange

Needle and syringe exchanges are key elements to harm reduction. By attracting the user through supplying clean equipment, they not only help prevent blood-borne diseases such as HIV and AIDS, but also help to maximise service user health.

Needle exchanges offer a supply of new injecting equipment including a range of syringes, disposal containers and condoms, together with advice on safer drug use and sex. They normally have easy access (ie, low threshold), and provide the opportunity for users to make use of other help such as counselling or legal advice.

Counselling and psycho-social therapies

The aim of counselling is to bring about behavioural change and to offer advice and information. Furthermore, counselling and other psychotherapeutic techniques are important constituent parts of many drug treatments. The techniques vary across and even within treatment programmes. They may range from fairly non-confrontational, and non-directional approaches where the counsellor or therapist seeks to help the client to understand and cope with their problems (many of which may be non-drug related), to more directional and/or confrontational techniques. Counselling tends to come in two forms:
- person centred, derived from Carl Rogers' approach
- cognitive behavioural, combining the principles of learning theory (behavioural theory) and cognition (knowledge and understanding used to control thoughts and behaviour).

Cognitive behavioural counselling is most commonly used in relapse prevention (stopping people returning to drug use) and motivational interviewing. Other counselling techniques include 12-step counselling, and relationship and family therapy. Often both individual and group (client's family and/or other clients) counselling/therapy is used.

Detoxification and methadone reduction

Simple detoxification helps the addict to overcome physical withdrawal symptoms and reach a point of drug-free existence. This can be done gradually or abruptly. While detoxification tries to eliminate the drugs from the body by using other drugs and therapies to maintain a bearable state of withdrawal, methadone reduction replaces the drug of choice, usually heroin, in ever-decreasing doses. The aim is to reduce each dose until the dose is stopped, usually over a period of six to eight weeks. There are also rapid opiate detoxification methods which involve heavy sedation. There are a number of drugs used, the most common being benzodiazepines or lofexidine, a drug with a detoxification action. Good quality support and aftercare services, tailored to the individual needs of the recovering addict, appear to be very important in determining the effectiveness of such treatment.

Maintenance prescribing

Maintenance programmes, where they exist, use a substitute drug such as methadone linctus, which is taken orally, to help prevent withdrawal symptoms and maintain a stable lifestyle. Other drugs are potentially available, but are rarely used – eg, injectable methadone, or heroin. The aim of the treatment is to stabilise and reduce the potential harm associated with illicit heroin use.

Heroin prescribing

Because of the well-publicised activities of a few doctors, there is a mistaken belief that heroin prescribing is an established part of current UK treatment policy. Very few doctors are licensed to prescribe heroin to addicts.

Treatment for stimulant drug use

Prescribing the drug of choice for amphetamine users is legally permissible, but the issue is a contentious one. On the one hand, advocates of prescribed amphetamine argue that in extreme cases, short-term maintenance is effective as a means of rapid stabilisation. On the other hand, GPs and drug agencies highlight the risks associated with continued amphetamine use and its inherent psychological and physical consequences.

Most agencies offer some form of limited amphetamine treatment such as counselling, referral to residential rehabilitation and alternative (not substitute) prescriptions – usually antidepressants.

The lack of specialist care also applies to those dependent on cocaine and crack. However, over the last decade, due to concerns about the increase of crack

8

use, agencies have responded by offering more specialised treatment for this group including counselling, cognitive behavioural therapy, and acupuncture and other complimentary therapies. Unlike amphetamine, the prescribing of cocaine to a chronic drug user requires a Home Office licence. Thus the only drug treatment likely to be offered to this type of user would be antidepressants.

Minnesota Model

Based originally on the principles of Alcoholics Anonymous, the Minnesota Model uses the 12-step model, usually with a strong religious element, to achieve total and sustained abstention from drugs. Steps one to five deal with changing the problem behaviours and beliefs of the client, while the remaining steps concentrate on sustaining abstinence and change. The principles are used across a range of delivery systems, though all seek the same aim. Mentoring is an important tool in acclimatising new clients to the process, preventing relapse and providing ongoing support.

Personal skills training

Some drug users may benefit from help in managing relationships, or stabilising a chaotic lifestyle through skills training. The training can be provided as part of a holistic structured day programme (see below) or customised to suit individual needs. A range of areas can be covered, such as:

- life-skills and vocational training
- building and restoring personal independence
- how to maintain links with families and social networks.

Skills training works best when it is provided as part of a care plan and co-ordinated with other treatment schemes – eg, counselling.

Alternative complementary therapies

There are a number of services which offer alternative therapies such as auricular acupuncture, homeopathic teas (which are used in the detoxification process and to aid sleep), meditation, reiki, yoga and shiatsu massage. Some may use alternative therapies as a compliment or exclusively when, for example, staving off cravings for stimulants.

What types of drug services are available?

The drugs field is large and diverse, and includes a range of statutory, private and voluntary sector services. The main types of services can be divided into two broad categories: *open access service* and those offering *structured care*.

Open access services

Community-based advice and information agencies

These are specialist agencies dealing exclusively with substance misuse providing advice and information to professionals as well as drug users, their families and friends.

Helplines

There are an increasing number of helplines for drug users, offering confidential advice on HIV, alcohol dependence, drug misuse, drug awareness, general information and counselling. The main service open to drug users is the **National Drugs Helpline** [Tel: 0800 776600], which offers 24-hour confidential advice and support. Others include **Drinkline** [Tel: 0845 601 4357], which offers the same for alcohol consumers and **ADFAM** [Tel: 020 7928 8900], which offers advice and counselling to users and their families. **Release** [Tel: 020 7603 8654] offers legal advice to users and has a special helpline for parents of children excluded from school for drug use.

Outreach

Reaching vulnerable or marginalised individuals is often a problem for support services. Outreach aims to contact hard-to-reach drug users by contacting people in the community. Outreach offers individual advice, and support and risk reduction interventions such as clean injecting equipment and condoms to those who would not normally come into contact with services. Outreach also offers peer education to encourage lower-risk behaviour.

The service comes in two forms:

- detached work, where workers go out into the users' own environment, such as clubs and homes
- institutional work, where the service works on site with other agencies such as health centres and schools.

Many of the institutional outreach projects have worked closely with other services and are able to put individuals in touch with appropriate help and advise on the local treatment facilities.

Needle and syringe exchange facilities

Needle and syringe exchange facilities are low threshold (informal and easy-access service) and accessible, offering many users their only contact with services. There are four types of exchange facilities:

- stand alone services
- those run from community-based services, either in-house or outreach services
- pharmacy-based schemes
- general practitioner services, run by GPs in surgeries.

Most community-based services offer needle exchange as part of their core work

8

and many offer exchange within the context of outreach into other generic services (peripatetic needle exchange). Some pharmacy and detached services use ready made packs for outreach type work. Most needle exchanges offer the chance to engage in other support such as advice and counselling, either on site or through a support network or coordinator.

Street agencies

These are locally-based agencies offering a range of services which might include a telephone helpline, drop-in centre, home visits and outreach (see above).

As well as information and advice (on *all* drugs), street agencies often provide individual and group counselling and other support services for those with drug problems and for those who are becoming, or who have become, abstinent from drugs. Many street agencies work closely with GPs, to provide primary health care and/or to provide prescriptions for withdrawal, detoxification and occasionally stabilisation through maintenance prescribing (see The types of help available, page 120). Street agencies can also provide harm reduction services, such as the provision of free condoms and safer sex advice/information, and needle/syringe exchanges and information and advice on safer injecting practices.

Self-help groups

Minnesota model

Groups such as Narcotics and Cocaine Anonymous (NA and CA) and Families Anonymous are two high-profile self-help groups based on the ideas of Alcoholics Anonymous, which essentially sees addiction as a lifelong disease from which there is never a complete cure. Therefore the only solution is total abstinence from any drugs or alcohol.

Narcotics Anonymous involves attendance at meetings, getting and providing mutual support from/to other members and adhering to the 12 steps towards a drug-free life. The encouragement to engage with a "power greater than ourselves" is explicit in the 12 steps to be practised. Formal religious adherence is not a necessary focus but may nonetheless figure strongly in some groups. Families Anonymous seeks to help families recognise problems that may be inherent in their functioning, which might contribute to the addict family member continuing with her/his addiction. It also has a 12-step programme for recovery.

There are other types of family and self-help groups offering advice, support and counselling – many of which operate from drug services.

Drug user support groups

Services managed by current and former users are becoming more common. Mainliners is one of the first, and was established by users suffering from HIV. The range of services provided differs, but many offer outreach, HIV prevention initiatives, drop-in with meals, individual and group counselling, alternative therapy, support groups, training events and newsletters.

Structured care services

1. Prescribing interventions

There are two types of prescribing interventions: community and in-patient.

Community prescribing

Specialist services are provided mainly by NHS trusts' secondary care services that deal exclusively with drug users. These include community drug teams (CDTs) and drug dependency units (DDUs).

Community drug teams represent the community arm of statutory provision. Services are similar to those offered by street agencies, although a drop-in service may not be available. CDTs may have close links with the DDU, and therefore access to clinical treatments (including psychiatric and psychological) through referral and liaison.

Drug dependency units are part of NHS provision, and as such are often located in hospitals, rather than in the community. Their range of services mirror many of those provided by street agencies, and they also provide various clinical treatments, such as detoxification through medium- and short-term prescribing. Most DDUs provide longer-term prescribing (mainly opiates) to stabilise those whom it is deemed appropriate. Maintenance prescribing is not normally offered, and some do not offer a prescription service at all. As might be expected in a clinical setting, psychiatric and psychological treatment is also available. Inpatient as well as outpatient detoxification may be available too.

GP-led services include prescribing services provided by primary care physicians and teams and include those GPs who are involved in a formal shared care scheme.

General practitioners Some GPs have a lot of experience of treating drug users while others tend to refer them to drug services. GPs can potentially offer a range of services relating to health problems associated with drug use, and also prescribe certain drugs for withdrawal, detoxification, stabilisation or maintenance. It is, however, evident from a number of surveys that most GPs consider the management of drug users and their problems as something that they would prefer to avoid.[2]

Shared care GPs have responsibility for the general health of drug users and are very often the first port of call for most individuals seeking help for their drug use; 70 per cent of those seeking help had first sought help from a GP. Shared care schemes enrol the services of local drug treatment services to help GPs identify specialist drug services, agree their roles and facilitate referral, assessment and management of a planned delivery of care taking a multi-disciplinary approach. , With the help of a liaison worker, a joint care plan is established for each client.

Pharmacists Many pharmacists provide clean needles through needle exchange schemes directly to users. While many prescribe substitute drugs, a minority offer supervised consumption, often in collaboration with specialist services or GPs.

8

2. Non-prescribing interventions
Residential services

Residential services are also referred to as residential rehabilitation units or rehabs. They are private or non-statutory services, and provide accommodation, food and support to help their clients become drug free. Rehabs are often located in areas well away from the temptations of inner-city life, although some local authorities require clients to be treated within their borders. Most of these services require the client to be drug free when entering the programme and prepared to become a committed part of a hierarchical community structure within which they learn to deal with a drug-free lifestyle through various individual and group support mechanisms. Clients may be able to self-refer, or may require a professional referral.

The services provided by rehabs can include: detoxification, ameliorative prescribing for crack-cocaine abstention, alternative therapies and other client-oriented interventions. Residential services often base their programmes on particular philosophies about drug addiction and what an individual must do to overcome it. Some of them, for example, are based on religious philosophies, others on psycho-therapeutic theories. Residency can vary, but usually lasts between two to eighteen weeks and can vary from highly intensive and structured to semi-supported living schemes similar to hostel accommodation. There are five types of residential rehabilitation units:

- residential therapeutic communities
- 12 step or Minnesota models
- general or Christian house
- semi-supported living schemes
- crisis intervention services.

Residential therapeutic communities (TCs) have their origins in at least two traditions: the Maxwell Jones approach (developed in England and providing behavioural or psychiatric help); and the Synanon, or Concept House, approach (developed in the USA). The Maxwell Jones approach tends to adopt a more democratic approach to rehab by encouraging residents to express their opinions. Both approaches encourage mutual support and confrontation in order to facilitate behavioural change. Rewards and privileges are used to encourage change.

12-step or Minnesota model is based on the principles of Alcoholics and Narcotics Anonymous (NA).[3] Reaching abstinence is a staggered process involving 12 steps to recovery. Drug use is seen as a disease, and total and continued abstinence the healed state. All are financially self-supporting.

Usually delivered as a short-term residential therapeutic programme, Minnesota model rehabs emphasise individual needs and include use of a multidisciplinary team of doctors, nurses, social workers, counsellors, psychologists, etc.[4] Attendance at NA meetings is integrated into the programme itself and is continued after residential treatment has ended.

General and Christian houses provide group and individual support. Participants are encouraged to take an active role in monitoring and shaping their therapy.

A Christian house programme may be run by Christian staff with or without any required religious structure. Where there is a specific religious requirement, those who are non-Christian or gay or lesbian may not be accepted. Those without a required religious structure, but run by Christian staff, offer group and individual support, and encourage participants to monitor and shape their therapy.

Semi-supported living schemes require clients to take some responsibility for their own recovery. Staff support tends to be provided for only 12 hours a day, encouraging clients to address their own needs within a semi-structured system.

Crisis intervention services offer immediate help and treatment. Although some interventions can be obtained from hospitals or psychiatric units, some residential services also provide dedicated crisis management for drug users. Access is immediate, residency usually lasts for one to two days, and a range of treatments is offered, including detoxification, primary health care, psychiatric assessment, food and rest, alternative therapies, legal, housing and social advice and support. Some may provide longer-term support with the option of referral.

Care planned counselling offers formal structured approaches with assessment, clearly defined treatment plans, treatment goals and regular reviews. They do not offer, as others do, advice and information, drop-in support and informal key working. Shared care is one example, but services other than GPs participate in care planned counselling.

Structured day programmes (SDPs) offer a structured approach to rehabilitation, working with a defined length of treatment programme. Clients are normally expected to attend four or five days a week, for several hours each day. SDPs offer advice, and sometimes counselling; almost all provide personal and skills training as well as access to other services and networks. Some use a rolling programme of activities where clients negotiate a timetable for their rehabilitation. Some programmes may accept current users as well as those who are drug free.

There are three types of SDPs:
- **12-step SDP**, which uses the first three steps of the Minnesota model
- **vocational SDP**, which teaches vocational skills such as literacy and numeracy skills, computer training, with some courses leading to National Vocational Qualifications
- **aftercare for residential rehabilitation**, using drop-in or drug-free accommodation that encourages attendance at vocational or training classes, to ease the transition into independent living.

Social inclusion or re-integration services

Housing advice and support services include systems to re-house drug users receiving treatment and those needing housing after rehabilitation. As well as offering

8

housing support, these services provide a network of care involving GPs, nurses, social workers and specialist drug service care. Such care tends to be brokered by a liaison worker who can identify risk factors associated with problem drug use and seek appropriate care to address a range of multiple needs.

Help within the prison or criminal justice system

One in five of those referred for treatment are in the criminal justice system, the same proportion as offenders within the system classified as problem drug users. A significant proportion of problem drug users, therefore, come into regular contact with the police and probation services.

Police

Arrest referral schemes, introduced in 1996, take advantage of the regular contact between police officers and drug users, to encourage the latter to seek support. Police can offer help ranging from the offer of contact numbers to on-site drug workers. Most schemes do not require those being approached to take up treatment, and although take-up rates appear to be low for the whole scheme (less than 50 per cent of those approached), those who accepted treatment appeared to benefit, with over half claiming to be drug free by the end of it.

Prisons

One of the key objectives of the *Prison Drug Strategy*[5] is to make drug services within the prison system more accessible and more like the range of services available on the outside. Prisons, therefore, are required to provide a set standard of care and reduce the harm caused by drug use.

Prison-based treatments

A range of in-house treatment services, advice, information and harm minimisation provisions are available to the drug user in the prison system. These include detoxification, counselling and 12-step programmes. However, at the moment clean needles are not provided, although some prisons provide sterilisation facilities. Most services are provided by prison staff or community-based drug agencies and commissioned by the Prison Service or as part of mainstream drug services.

Prison doctors are able to refer prisoners to services provided either in-house or by institutional workers. In the majority of cases, take-up of treatment is voluntary. However, the introduction of drug treatment orders and mandatory drug testing means that prisoners can be required to take up treatment within the system or on probation. If this is done, individuals have to present themselves for assessment and take up a prescribed treatment regime.

Help is often available to remand and sentenced prisoners. Since October 1999, nearly all prison drug services are provided through the CARATS framework (see below).

Drug Treatment and Testing Orders (DTTOs)

DTTOs aim to break the link between problematic drug use and crime (see Chapter 5), by supervising offenders with drug problems and implementing and monitoring drug treatment under sentence. Under a DTTO, an offender is required to undertake treatment to reduce or eliminate their drug use as part of their community sentencing. Lasting from six months to three years, DTTOs can involve a range of treatments, including residential and detoxification. DTTOs require the consent of the offender. Although similar to probation orders 1A(6), DTTOs differ in three ways. Firstly, courts retain the sentence throughout its length by holding regular reviews. Secondly, regular or random urine tests are administered to monitor progress. Thirdly, changes to sentencing is permitted in response to progress or problems.

CARATS

The provision of help and throughcare of prisoners is founded in all prisons on the CARATS framework (Counselling, Assessment, Referral, Advice and Throughcare Services). The scheme provides low level intervention for prisoners with low to moderate drug problems and aims to:

- identify (problem) drug users as soon as possible
- provide ongoing support and advice while in prison
- in partnership with internal and external agencies, assess and engage prisoners in appropriate help where needed
- link various departments and agencies involved in dealing with prisoners, including prison officers, medical staff, psychologists, specialist drug workers and probation officers to create the CARATS team
- provide continuity between treatment in prison and that available on release.

Entrance into a CARATS scheme can occur at any stage of a sentence or remand. Prisoners can self-refer, although most are referred following a reception interview, a medical assessment, or a positive Mandatory Drugs Test (MDT) (see Chapter 7). Care is generally overseen by the prison's drugs strategy co-ordinator. Direct care and care planning is undertaken by an allocated CARATS worker, who will meet, assess and monitor the progress of the prisoner. Probation officers take the lead role in throughcare arrangements.

Probation

The core of probation work is to prevent reoffending, and part of that work is to minimise the problems caused by drug use. Probation services have good contacts with local health authorities and street agencies, and can refer individuals to appropriate services and treatment. They also play an important role in supervising care and reporting to courts prior and after sentencing, overseeing the management of care and the participation of the user, and providing information and support in the form of housing and benefits. Throughcare may also be available, often forming part of a CARATS care plan, which obliges the prison and

8

probation service to continue treatment of the individual, by retaining contact with outside agencies and close family, and, importantly, making provision for care and treatment on release.

Help for specific groups

Most of the services covered so far are aimed at adult, often white, male, opiate users. However, increasing recognition is being given to the problematic use of different drugs and different users. In this section we look at services for young people and families, black and minority ethnic groups, stimulant users, those with co-existing mental illness, and people with blood-borne diseases.

Young people

Most services are ill-equipped to deal with needs of young people (defined as anyone under the age of 18). Services for young people should operate within the Children Act 1989, which entails partnership work with local Area Child Protection Committees and social services children and families teams, along with other relevant child-focussed agencies. The parents or guardians of the young person should also be involved where possible, although treatment may be provided without parental consent in certain situations. Unlike services for adults, treatment services for young people are not able to provide a fully confidential service, as sharing information with social services may be good practice in certain child protection situations. Other young people's services, such as needle exchanges, may not be provided without full assessment and further intervention where possible.

Other developments are currently leading towards integrated children's services, able to address multiple needs and vulnerabilities. Children's Service Plans will encompass various coexisting service plans, such as a youth justice plan, a drug action plan. The Connexions Service will provide a personal adviser for every young person aged 13-19 who will broker access to services and liaise with schools, parents and primary and other carers.

Women

Women tend to have different histories and patterns of problematic drug use and display different needs and characteristics. Women may also have childcare issues. Women tend also respond better to single-gender support groups. Pregnant women also have specific needs.

Pregnant users

Some services provide maternity liaison services. These aim to provide advice and care to the pregnant user and to prevent possible obstetric complications. The services, in providing a liaison nurse, act as a focal point between drug and alcohol services, antenatal services and health visitors. Some provide a special clinic service for pregnant women and their partners. More recently, training of generic staff to deal with the needs of pregnant users is being adopted, offering a more holistic approach to drug treatment.

Residential care for women

Some rehab units provide residential care for women who need help with their drug use as well as other problems such as sexual abuse and childcare issues. Others target particular groups of women. The Bethany Project in London, for example, provides care for women who work or have worked in the sex industry. Treatments offered vary, but may include assertiveness training, financial, housing and childcare support, understanding and combating eating disorders and safe house provision.

Families

Nearly all services for relatives and carers are based in the non-statutory sector. ADFAM provides information, counselling and advice at a national level, including a help-line and training for family support groups. At a local level, some rehabilitation units provide residential services to couples or parents and their children. Street agencies may also provide advice and counselling to parents and families.

Black and minority ethnic groups

Some drug agencies actively target black drug users by having ratios of black and minority ethnic staff and positive multi-cultural images. Others run black drug users groups and provide outreach work into black and Asian communities. There are also agencies solely dedicated to black and minority ethnic groups, such as the Asian prescribing services in London.

Stimulant users

There is increasing recognition of the special needs associated with stimulant use, mainly crack-cocaine and amphetamine. These include ameliorative prescribing regimes, alternative therapies such as acupuncture, relapse prevention and stress management techniques. Structured day programmes are available, as are support groups for female crack users.

Co-existence of mental health illness

Despite the use of simple terms such as dual diagnosis, those with substance use and mental health problems are a diverse group, presenting a variety of specific problems. In many areas, particularly metropolitan areas, these clients may be homeless and/or involved in the criminal justice system. Up to 90 per cent of those with drug use problems in the criminal justice system are believed to have mental health problems. Lack of a clear definition of dual diagnosis and diversity of need has meant that services react in very different ways to the needs of such clients. There are, however, some needs which can be identified:

- Clients often 'slip through the net'. There is therefore a need to maintain intense supervision through frequent contacts between all professionals, carers and

8

agencies.

- Engaging clients is often very difficult. Clients often need domiciliary visits or reimbursement of travel costs, practical help and advice on other matters.
- Clients often lack important skills and require education and skills training to maximise daily functioning ability. Clients benefit from various skills training such as relapse prevention, anxiety management, symptom recognition and medical management, assertiveness and social skills training.
- Clients often have a range of needs spanning housing to legal help. Accessing help from agencies such as housing, social, therapeutic and legal organisations often helps facilitate understanding of client needs within these services.
- Their lives can often be chaotic. Structured low key programmes such as low threshold methadone maintenance programmes are of more benefit in reducing chaos than intense therapeutic sessions.

There is increasing recognition that special treatment services for clients with co-existing mental illness can exacerbate exclusion. Services therefore are increasingly providing training to specialist drug staff to help deal with clients with mental health problems, and conversely, mental health staff are being given training on how to deal with drug use problems. In this way, clients are included in mainstream care and service provision.

Therapies available include relapse prevention techniques, brief intervention therapy, 12-step philosophy, updated drug and alcohol information, motivational interviewing techniques and so on, to increase knowledge, skills and confidence.

Blood-borne diseases

Drug users with blood-borne diseases such as HIV, AIDS or Hepatitis C require not only clean needles, prescribing, counselling and other support, but also they often require intense medical and social care specific to their illness. Projects such as Mainliners offer respite care (short-term care for patients while their main carer has a break) and terminal care for those with AIDS. Many drug services, because of these needs, employ a specialist HIV worker. Over half of residential units have health-related services for such clients, and have specific group work and counselling, usually provided in liaison with local specialist organisations or medical centres. Special diets are often provided, as are information and advice sessions, as well as tests and vaccinations (hepatitis C) if requested. Some units also provide special emergency leaving packs containing details of the nearest syringe exchange schemes for those leaving unexpectedly.

What is a good service and what works?
Quality standards
QuADS

Standards for care and treatment is set by QuADS (Quality in Alcohol and Drug Services). As well as publishing a guidance manual on setting and monitoring standards,[6] the service aims to:

- identify key indicator quality standards for minimum, desirable and enhanced standards of alcohol and drug service provision for generic and target group services
- design a programme of support and training for alcohol and drug services to enable them to implement the standards
- identify and pilot standards for assessing competencies of individual workers in alcohol and drug services.

National Drug Treatment Agency

In July 2000 the government announced the launch of the National Drug Treatment Agency. It is understood that the agency will oversee the administration of drug treatment, co-ordinate funding and adopt and enforce standards for treatment services. At present, the majority of treatment is co-ordinated and funded locally in accordance with local drug action plans and service requirements.

What works?

Raistrick and Davidson[7] asked the important question 'does treatment work?' The question was deemed to be worth asking because although we can see that various treatment programmes have a certain amount of success, we also have to recognise that treatment often does not appear to succeed to any greater degree than no treatment. This is because much drug use, problematic or not, actually ends after an indeterminate period of time.

The question of success is important. This is because drug users may have preconceptions about what they need and expect from a service, service providers may have preconceptions about what should be provided, and funding for services may increasingly come to rely on statistics demonstrating the effectiveness of a service. If an expensive drug treatment facility is to be judged in terms of cure alone, then many services will be under threat, and as we have seen, some programmes do not even have abstinence as their primary aim. So what should be seen as successful treatment? Perhaps the question should be 'can drug addicts be successfully helped?'

The National Treatment Outcome Research Study (NTORS) asks this very question. Commissioned in 1994, NTORS provides information on the long-term effectiveness of four treatment modalities: methadone maintenance programmes, methadone reduction programmes, residential rehabilitation programmes, and specialist in-patient drug dependence units. The data also forms part of the key performance indicator for monitoring the reduction of levels of crime committed to pay for drug misuse, set out as a main strategic objective by the government.

The latest paper[8] presents six-month treatment outcomes for patients who received community-based methadone treatment in either a specialist drug clinic or a general practice setting. A multi-site follow-up study of treatment outcome was conducted with 452 opiate addicts who had been given methadone treatment in primary health care and specialist clinic settings. Outcome data are presented

8

8

for substance use behaviours, health, and crime.

Of those who were injecting at intake, the percentage sharing equipment fell from 33 per cent to 14 per cent for residential clients, and from 22 per cent to 12 per cent for non-residential clients. Abstinence rates increased, fewer clients were using regularly and there were improvements in terms of quantity used. Improvements in terms of alcohol use were not so marked however.

Improvements in drug-related problems, health, and social functioning were found at follow-up among both the GP and the clinic-treated groups. Problems at intake were broadly comparable among the clinic-based and the GP patients. Similar levels and types of improvement were also found for both groups at six-month follow-up.

Results demonstrate the feasibility of treating opiate addicts using methadone in primary health care settings, and show that treatment outcomes for such patients can be as satisfactory as for patients in specialist drug clinics. The GPs in the study are unrepresentative in their willingness to be actively involved with problem drug users moreover, several services treated relatively large numbers of drug users.

Harm reduction

Harm reduction interventions include the provision of new injecting equipment for drug injectors, the teaching of safer injecting behaviour, safer-sex advice, and provision of free condoms. Such services enable users to access help at will and under their own conditions, therefore offering help to a range of users in a variety of states or stages of use and who may not access services otherwise.

The provision of clean needles in preventing the spread of HIV and AIDS is an example of the efficacy of harm reduction techniques.

1. Branigan P, Kuper H & Wellings K (1997) *Posterspotting: The evaluation of the London dance safety campaign.* London: London School of Hygiene and Tropical Medicine.
2. Glanz A (1994) 'The fall and rise of the general practitioner', in Strang, J and Gossop, M *Heroin Addiction and Drug Policy: The British system*, Oxford: Oxford Medical Publications.
3. Curson D A (1991) 'Private Treatment of alcohol and drug problems in Britain', editorial, *British Journal of Addiction*, 86, p 9-11.
4. Ibid.
5. HM Prison Service (1998) *Tackling Drugs in Prison: The Prison Service drug strategy*, London: HMSO.
6. Standing Conference on Drug Abuse (1999) *QuADS*, London: DrugScope.
7. Raistrick D & Davidson R J (1985) *Alcoholism and Drug Addiction*, Churchill Livingstone.
8. Gossop M, Marsden J, Stewart D, Lehmann P & Strang J (1999) 'Methadone treatment practices and outcome for opiate addicts treated in drug clinics and in general practice: results from the National Treatment Outcome Research Study', *British Journal of General Practice* 49 (438), p 31-4.

drugs

& the media

9

TEXT | **ROSS COOMBER**

YOUR | QUESTIONS | **ANSWERED**

What type of images of drugs and drug users does the media portray? | What are

media education campaigns? | Why do different drug articles say the same thing? |

What is the impact of media reporting on attitudes to drugs and drug users? | What

are moral panics? | Why does the media present such images?

Introduction

This chapter will briefly review and explore the relationship between drugs and the media. It is not intended to be exhaustive nor does it seek to provide more than an introduction to many of the issues raised.

The relationship is not a simple one. Messages about drugs are often mixed and contradictory, and people do not receive messages from the media passively, simply accepting the views of journalists and politicians without reference to their own experience and beliefs. This situation is further complicated when we consider the *role* of the media. Is it there to inform, to reflect the views of the population, or to stimulate serious debate? It has also been argued that the media is manipulated into playing up and exaggerating drug issues to move the focus away from other sensitive topics, such as unemployment and poverty (Goode and Ben-Yehuda, 1994; Kohn, 1987; Edelman, 1988). These issues will be considered below.

What type of images of drugs and drug users does the media portray?

"The day I saw drugs kill my sister" (*Daily Mail*, 4.3.00)
"Janice Joplin's Story: her fatal addiction to drugs, sex and rock'n'roll" (*Daily Mail*, 6.3.00)
"Cannabis in heart attack alert" (*Express*, 3.3.00)

Each of these headlines are examples of how, in just one month, the national tabloid and local press commonly build up stories related to drugs and/or drug users. The headlines are powerful and succinct, sticking to the commonly perceived dangers of drugs and what happens if you get mixed up with them. Drug stories are considered by the media to be newsworthy, at least in the sense that they are judged to be of such popular interest that they will attract audiences or readers. But it is not just newspapers and magazines which have a consistent interest. Drug-related themes are also the stuff of many films, documentaries, chat shows, commercials (government health education campaigns), and television soap operas. Overwhelmingly they tend to present a variation on the images evoked by the headlines above.

It is true however that depending on the medium involved (television, magazines, broadsheet newspapers, tabloids), the approach will tend to vary even if the general message does not. So, for example, a recent report on an ex-steroid user who committed suicide by running head first into a wall while resident in a psychiatric ward was headlined on the front page of the national tabloid *Today* as "Steroids Drove Him Mad… then Mr Muscles killed himself". In the local newspaper, the front page kept up the drug connection with the headline, "Emotional plea by mother of bodybuilder driven mad by steroid abuse" (*South London Press* 10.3.95). By contrast, *The Guardian* devoted only a small column to the story headed "Man Died After Butting Wall" but then uncritically reported that the individual had used steroids and that this had been cited as sufficient cause. In fact it is by no means certain that the 'quality' broadsheet newspapers are necessarily more reliable, for as Bean (1993, p 61) has pointed out, in relation to reporting around crack cocaine, "The *Observer* had consistently been the source of some of the most dramatic forms of presentation and indeed misinformation, even overtaking some of the tabloids... crack was described as "a highly refined and smokable variant of cocaine, said to be so potent that a single dose can lead to addiction... this drug crack is a killer. And Britain could be its next target in the 1980s".

Most drug-related stories, like those above, do not try to present the story within a broader context or question its facts but are happy to blame the drug as sole cause. No consideration, for example, was given in these stories to the body-builder's previous psychiatric disposition or, in the case of crack, whether the reports were consistent with what we know about addiction and the effects of cocaine in general. Assumptions therefore are made about drug effects and their harmful potential which are neither substantiated nor questioned. It is as though there is an underlying assumption that we already know as much as we need to know about drugs and their effects and about drug users and the things they are capable of. This is often taken to its logical conclusion by the common use of drug user biographies –"At nine he was in the playground, at 12 he was sniffing glue, at 22 my son Georgie was dead from an overdose" (*Daily Mirror* 17.10.94), the unquestioned quoting/interviewing of an ex-drug user or someone close to them – "Once they take it they're hooked for life. People who sell these drugs are murderers and they are evil" (*Guardian* 22.1.94, quoting the distressed mother of a dead heroin addict) or reference to what is often unsubstantiated fact – "Highly addictive and easily obtainable, crack is the fastest growing problem on the drug scene. You may think you can handle it but after one high you are hooked, as 22-year-old student Michele discovered" (*Mazz,* May 1994).

Drug stories can be so useful to certain reporting that even when the drug connection is tenuous to the main story it is not unusual for the drug aspect to be given undue and often misleading prominence. For example, the story that ran under the heading "Drugs Kill Def Leppard Rock Idol Steve" (*Today* 1991), actually reported that the musician died from alcohol poisoning not a drug overdose. Similarly, the headline "Teenager Kim Armitage died after a cocktail of drink and drugs..." (*Daily Express* 1995) arguably suggested use of illicit drugs whereas the drugs in question were in fact "aspirin with her mother's painkillers". Messner *et al* (1993) illustrate how a story about wife battering in two major daily newspapers framed it as a drugs story while largely ignoring the violence aspect.

Some stories carry with them widely held assumptions about street drugs that journalists feel able to cite with impunity, despite almost no evidence: "Ecstasy has turned to agony for thousands of E users as dealers spike tablets and capsules with heroin, LSD, *rat poison and crushed glass* [my emphasis]" (*Time Out* 27.10.93). Although firmly believed even by many drug agency workers and users themselves, the existence of rat poison or crushed glass as adulterants in street drugs is almost unheard of (see Chapter 10).

9

Statistics provide another potentially misleading source about the drug scene, when "Official statistics are swallowed whole [and] where official/expert (or not so expert) statements are uncritically treated as reality" (Shapiro 1981).

What are media education campaigns?

There are often many factual inaccuracies and distortions in media reporting of drugs. For example, in portraying heroin use, popular media in particular will revert to stereotypical images of the heroin user as being invariably spotty, skinny, ill and deceitful, living a life of unremitting crime and degradation leading to the mortuary slab. This view of heroin use was adopted wholesale by the government's 1985/6 and 1987 drug education campaigns which used conventional scare tactics in an attempt to prevent young people trying drugs. No more is this evident than in a recent campaign in January 2000 by Barnardos, which used heroin use as means for shocking people. In asking why a young man injects heroin due to a lack of care early on in his life, the poster shows a baby injecting himself with heroin while sitting in his own faeces in a dirty back street. The combination of a young vulnerable baby and drug use is a common tool for eliciting horror, sympathy and abhorrence.

These campaigns were deliberate attempts to use the media as a tool for preventing drug use, by communicating the potential horrors of heroin addiction. While not being wrong (in the sense that the images can and do represent the *consequences* of heroin use in many instances), they are unhelpful as a way of understanding much about drug use and addiction.

One obvious consequence of these media campaigns was that media reporting of drugs in the more sensationalist forms already discussed was given added credibility. Interestingly, there was anecdotal evidence that some young people found the emaciated image of the boy in the 1987 poster campaign accompanying the TV adverts rather attractive, and used the poster to decorate their bedrooms. The actual research conducted to evaluate the impact of the campaigns indicated that those who were anti-heroin in the first place had their feelings confirmed by the campaign, but there was nothing to indicate that any sort of scare campaign would actually stop somebody experimenting with the drug.

One unintended effect of scare campaigns, which give such massive prominence and visibility to drugs such as heroin, is that they may actually *increase* experimentation with these drugs. In its 1984 report *Prevention* (pp 35-36), the government's own advisory body, the Advisory Council on the Misuse of Drugs (ACMD) warned, "Whilst we accept the need, in appropriate circumstances, for education to include factual information about drugs and their effects, we are concerned about measures which deliberately present information in a way which is intended to shock or scare. We believe that educational programmes based on such measures on their own are likely to be ineffective or, at the very worst, positively harmful". Research elsewhere has supported this fear (De Haes, 1987; Schaps *et al*, 1981). Thus, for some young people, branding the use of mysterious and dangerous substances as antisocial and deviant may (especially if they have seen peers using these drugs with few of the effects sensationalised by the media) provide a focus and new outlet through which their frustrations may be vented and their resistance demonstrated, while for others it may merely spark their curiosity.

Why do drug articles sound the same?
The language of drug reporting

When it comes to presenting the drug issue to the public there is a common vocabulary with recurrent metaphors informing the statements and reports, not only of the press but also national and local politicians, medical experts, and many others. Two of the most consistent metaphors are the drug 'epidemic' – the disease running unchecked across the land contaminating all it touches – and the 'war' against drugs where gung-ho language such as 'fight', 'battle', and 'onslaught on the drugs epidemic' (all from one story, *Evening Standard* 22.4.94) is used to reassure the public that the sternest possible law and order response is in place to deal with the problem.

The notion of an epidemic is useful because it evokes an image of contamination that cannot be controlled except by the harshest measures – segregation, incarceration, kill or cure. An epidemic is a public health issue, affecting us all. It is not a problem of individuals, but of communities and society. The metaphor completely removes from the picture the active individual, the circumstances under which initial drug experimentation takes place and the context in which continued use is likely to occur – that is, it de-personalises the problem. Epidemics can also be forecast to achieve all sorts of worrying proportions, and, as we shall see later in relation to crack, be exaggerated out of all proportion to the actual problem.

By using and repeating particular metaphors it has been argued that 'reality' is framed and organised in particular ways, "For example, framing the issue of drug abuse… by using the 'drug war' metaphor implies a strong application of law enforcement and even military intervention to the problem" (McLeod et al 1992), as has happened in the USA (Trebach 1987). On the other hand, a differing emphasis on addiction as a health problem rather than a social one, may frame the issue differently and consequently lead to a helpful response instead of a criminal justice one. There was evidence of both these approaches in the UK during the mid-1980s. Concern over the rise in the number of young heroin addicts (seen as victims who needed help) ran parallel to the more traditional reporting about drug traffickers (seen as 'evil merchants of doom' who needed locking up). Thus the media helped create the climate where substantial new resources were made available for treatment and rehabilitation, at the same time as restating the public demand for a 'war against drugs' directed at traffickers.

9

What is the impact of media reporting on attitudes to drugs and drug users?

The oldest debates about the press have centred around its ability to influence people's thinking and attitudes. This debate remains relevant to the drug issue. If most media portrayals of drugs tend to reproduce existing drug mythologies, fail to contextualise drug issues more broadly, and sensationalise much of the experience of drug use in society, then we need to consider how important this is to how drug use is generally understood and dealt with.

However, trying to actually determine the impact of the press on attitudes to particular issues is far from easy. Certainly, the aptly named 'hypodermic syringe model' – which has it that audiences are directly and predictably influenced by the media, information being pumped into the body of the population and absorbed – is inappropriate in this case. On the other hand, many surveys about drugs show that most people's main source of information about drugs is the popular media (Coggans, 1991).

Most media output is intended to be informative or entertaining. Research that has attempted to find out how much the media can inform and educate, and therefore alter or even reinforce existing beliefs, has shown that media effects are complex. Different status, class, gender and cultural groups receive information differently and do different things with it (Morley, 1980; Tichenor *et al*, 1970; Cantril, 1940). Despite this complexity, there are a number of areas where media influence appears able to have impacts that are relevant to our discussion.

Firstly and most obviously, the general public is unusually dependent on the media for information about any new phenomenon (Katz & Lazarsfeld, 1955; Glover, 1984). A recent example of this, the emergence of HIV/AIDS in the early 1980s, led to all sorts of negative images and press sensationalism ('gay plague') providing false messages and information that proved difficult to dislodge, even from some health care workers years after more reliable information was known. This also indicates that initial and fearful images may in some cases be relatively resistant to future alternative messages.

Secondly, it's hardly surprising that existing views and attitudes are easily reinforced, particularly because of the cumulative exposure to similar images in newspapers, television, books and films going back decades. What is significant is that alternative messages, although they occasionally surface, are comfortably countered by the weight of messages that reinforce existing perceptions. This is particularly true when combined with a topic or subject upon which individuals are almost entirely reliant on the media for their information. Finally, the language and metaphors used by the media may help frame the way a problem is seen and help set the agenda for how it should be dealt with.

What are moral panics?

One further recurrent theme around drugs and the media is that of the 'moral panic' or the media-led drug scare. In this scenario, the media are able to create a scare through the reporting of drug-related concerns disproportionately to the actual seriousness of the problem. Scares may originate from an increase in Customs and Excise drug seizures or the arrival of a 'new' drug. The theory of the moral panic was originally developed by Stan Cohen (1972) in relation to the fears around violence between mods and rockers in the 1960s. Cohen sought to explain how a relatively small and isolated social problem (a clash of the two groups in a seaside town over a bank holiday weekend) was exaggerated in the media to something more. The stories were spiced up with the negative imagery of leather jackets and motorbike gangs, suggesting that the seriousness of the incident was actually related to the type of individual involved and the fear that such behaviour and fashions among the young would become a broad threat to society as a whole. The consequences of a moral panic are that it creates an amplification spiral, with the police, courts, government and the general public becoming less tolerant of the behaviour depicted. Similar styles, fashions and images often get sucked into the vortex and an isolated incident becomes more broadly defined. This results in the creation of new social controls (eg, laws, restrictions) constructed as a response to the problem as conceived. Explicit in most theories of moral panic is the idea that the focus of the panic (the group involved) serves to identify folk-devils (eg, junkies) who are then scapegoated as examples of what is wrong with society and who provide a target onto which general fears and anxieties may be pinned.

The crack cocaine scare of the late 1980s occurred during an ongoing anti-drugs (predominately heroin) campaign, and resulted in what Bean (1993, p 59) describes as a drug scare without parallel in all those that have "beset the British drug scene over the last 25 years". This was despite the fact that little evidence was available of any significant increase in use in Britain. The scare elicited overstatement from all quarters – neither the quality press, television news nor tabloids were immune. Bean (1993) similarly suggests that the crack scare in Britain was media-*led*, based on speculative assumptions about instant addiction, a ready and existing demand, and the notion that problems which emerge in the USA have a strong likelihood of surfacing here. The epidemic never happened and the National Task Force set up to outmanoeuvre and deal with the expected problem was disbanded two-and-a-half years later through relative inactivity. It was, however, indicative of what the media could do with a drug issue. US drug enforcement agents forecast a crack explosion in Britain and hyped the drug as having previously unseen powers. The media chose not to question the reliability of these predictions but to accept them unconditionally. The situation in Britain in 2000 is that crack does have a significant presence in areas of traditional drug use, such as deprived inner-city areas, and does cause many problems. However, the dire predictions about the end of British society as we know it have thankfully not been proved correct.

9

The impact of panics on public attitudes is borne out by research. Reeves and Campbell (1994) relate how in the USA in the mid-1980s the media-led crack scare helped produce a jump in public opinion on drugs as the nation's most important problem from 2% to 13% over the five month period of mass coverage. Beckett (1994) has described how public fears and anxieties over crime and drugs are often transformed by panics led and constructed by the media, and others have described similar media-inspired drug scares elsewhere, especially in America (Goode & Ben-Yehuda, 1994; Trebach, 1987; Reinerman & Levine, 1989).

Why does the media present such images?

So far we have looked at the type of drug-related images presented in the media and considered how useful they are as a means of understanding drug use. We then considered the effects of these representations and found that although effects as such are difficult to measure there are circumstances where they are more likely to occur, such as when new information becomes available. We also have to recognise that in general, the media (or at least the *news* media) is aware that it can influence attitudes and behaviour and accordingly tries to reflect that responsibility in the manner of its information provision. We then have to ask *why* does the news media report drugs in the way that it does? At the very least, there appear to be three interrelated factors that may partly explain how and why such reporting has come to pass: the construction of 'the dope fiend', the importance of the 'human-interest' story, and the view that the media acts as a 'mirror' to society.

The dope fiend

For much of the 19th century there was little concern over the very common use of opium and it was taken widely as a form of self-medication for a wide range of ailments. From the 1830s a number of factors came together that fundamentally altered public perceptions of opium and the type of person who used it. Fears were soon raised about the displacement of alcohol by opium amongst the working classes and its use for stimulation rather than for medication. Such use was considered as a societal threat despite little or no evidence to support this belief (Berridge and Edwards 1987).

These fears later coincided with, and were bolstered by, the claims of the emerging medical and pharmaceutical professions that opium was too dangerous a drug to be available for self-medication and that there should be controls (medical and pharmaceutical, of course) over its use. This came about because of genuine concerns over the rise in the number of infant poisonings, but opium and other drugs also became the battleground over which doctors and pharmacists fought for control of the prescription of drugs.

There was also a much more unpleasant concern – that of a perceived threat to society from outside – ie, xenophobia. From the 1860s, interest grew in the numerically small but highly-concentrated and visible Chinese immigrant population in London. And as far as the media of the time was concerned, wherever there was a

Chinaman, there was an opium den. Literature was riddled with the drug and its effects, from Dickens's *Mystery of Edwin Drood* (1870) to Oscar Wilde's *Picture of Dorian Gray* (1891) and Conan Doyle's Sherlock Holmes stories. Opium smoking was depicted in these books "in a manner soon accepted as reality… 'fantastic postures on ragged mattresses. The twisted limbs, the gaping mouths, the staring lustreless eyes'… Not all writers were so obviously hostile; yet from the 1870s an increasing tone of racial and cultural hostility was discernible" (Berridge and Edwards 1987, p 197). Opium was blamed for the failure of missionaries to convert the Chinese to Christianity, and the use of opium for pleasure became linked to depravity and weakness. The ever-present Victorian fear of 'racial contamination' was only heightened by the newly-perceived fear of opium.

Similar issues had also emerged in the USA in the 1870s, where there was a much larger Chinese population. Kohn (1992, p 2) notes that "Variations on this scene set the tone of the British drug panic of the 1920s, firing on the potent juxta-position of young white women, 'men of colour' [the term was current], sex and drugs. If the ultimate menace of drugs had to be summarised in a single proposi-tion, it would be that they facilitated the seduction of young white women by men of other races". Between 1910 and 1930 Parssinen (1983) reports "In newspapers, fiction and films, the public was deluged with a mass of fact and opinion about . drugs. The perception of danger expressed in… the previous four decades, gave way to near hysteria" (p 115). In the USA other racist images of blacks, Mexicans and Chinese were being spread by zealots such as Hamilton Wright who propagat-ed stories about black cocaine users who, once intoxicated, raped white women and could only be halted by a hail of bullets (Musto, 1987). In England, headlines demonstrated similar fears: "White Girls 'Hypnotised' by Yellow Men", "The Lure of the Yellow Man – English Girls' Moral Suicide – Fatal Fascination" (Kohn, 1992, p 3). With the First World War furnishing reporters with the opportunity to com-bine drug scare stories with those of alien conspiracies and spies (Kohn 1992), the construction of the drug fiend and the powers of dope were as firmly entrenched as the troops in France.

In the USA in the 1930s, it was the turn of other drugs to be demonised. Harry Anslinger, head of the newly-formed Narcotics Bureau, saw drug use as deplorable and degenerate but, more importantly, needed a "good drug scare" to keep funds coming in from the US Congress. Anslinger's descriptions of the effects of cannabis seem astounding to us now, but as Gossop (1993) observes they also sat-isfied a need: "The smallest dose, he told his eager audience, was likely to cause fits of raving madness, sexual debauchery, violence and crime". 'Scientific' evidence such as this, presented by a highly-placed US official, did much to exacerbate how drugs (even comparatively benign ones like cannabis) came to be viewed by the media. The descriptions of addicts at times read like science fiction, but these descriptions came from law courts (Wisotsky, 1991), public officials and doctors, not from Martians. In the decades that followed, the connection between drugs and 'others' (foreigners) or 'outsiders' (deviants) was continuously reinforced (Bean 1974) and often acted as a catalyst for action against drug users.

9

9

The dope fiend had been born, and once such reporting was underway (and it would have been deemed proper and responsible to inform the public of such evils), the familiar media stereotypes became set in stone. They then became increasingly reliant on the framework employed in the reporting of human interest stories and the problems attendant in that reporting.

Human interest stories

Curran *et al* (1980, p 306) have argued that human interest stories, are a type showing that life is "strongly governed by luck, fate, and chance [and] shares common universal experiences: birth, love, death, accident, illness, and, crucially, the experience of consuming". They seek to reach the maximum audience through appealing to the lowest common denominator; they "cross the barriers of sex, class and age, appealing almost equally to all types of reader" (p 301). This, they argue, is true of the so-called quality papers as well as the tabloids. A similar approach can be seen even in highly-regarded news programmes, such as the News at Ten, which recently introduced an 'And finally...' section into its broadcasting. This explicitly attempts to end a normal broadcast of doom and gloom (unemployment, civil wars, famines etc) with a happy, light-hearted human interest story. Typical human interest stories are looking to hook the audience, with a certain amount of professional licence applied to the material and its presentation. Curran argues that commercial pressure since the early 1920s has led to a particular style of news reporting that needs to attract attention and appeal. Drugs stories are only one of many topics (along with sex, crime, scandal and dead donkeys) which are considered to do both. Drugs issues fit neatly into the human interest story formula, even (as we have seen) turning stories which may have little saleable interest into drug stories in an effort to spice them up and increase audiences.

Whose media is it anyway?

The six-million dollar question has to be 'who controls the media' – whose views does it reflect? Sometimes the answer is easy. In the Soviet Union the media was state-run and most of its presentations paid homage to the ideas and propaganda of the Communist Party (Lane, 1990). But in democratic societies like Britain and the US the debate continues over whether media output is independent, supportive of capitalist ideas, influenced and manipulated by government or by media tycoons. The debate is too lengthy and contorted to repeat here but one aspect, the idea of the media as mirror, is important.

In relation to a subject like drugs, this would suggest that for the most part the media provides us with images and perspectives which are in line with reasoned public and authoritative thinking, and is therefore responsibly acting in the public interest. And indeed, much of what the media is itself fed in the form of press releases, public comment, and government campaigns contain images that are not inconsistent with what the media then passes on to us. In this sense, the media may be said to be providing legitimate and responsible images and, rather than trying to agitate and challenge what is a general consensus on drugs, merely reflects what people already believe. If this is true (and it undoubtedly is in part) then – when combined with the reporting style of the human interest story and the dope fiend stereotype – we can begin to understand why so many drug stories take the form they do and why they continue to do so.

We might also note that recent research has shown that the UK print media has no quality control mechanisms regarding the reporting of drug-related issues in operation (Coomber et al, 2000) and believes that good journalistic practice will itself ensure that reporting on drugs is objective and well-researched. Unfortunately, given the tenor of much media reporting and its common failure to engage with scientific research even on the most basic of issues such as drug-related risk, mortality, the nature of addiction and drug effects in general, we need to strongly question the efficacy of journalistic practice in this regard.

Conclusions

Obviously there are many dangers and problems associated with drug use but the media consistently represents them in ways which distort and fail to adequately contextualise them. This in turn often results in misleading and uninformative images and text.

Why should this matter? Shouldn't people have the worst possible image of drugs? Putting aside the ethical issue of misleading the public, one of the main problems with scare tactics is the impact they have on drug users and the way they may be treated by family, police, the courts and employers. It may, for example, prevent them and their families seeking help because of the stigma attached to drug use.

At present the relationship between drugs and the media is not a good one and is a simplistic one, cast in black and white terms. If the role of the media is in any sense to live up to the ideal where "access to relevant information affecting the public good is widely available, where discussion is free… [and where] the media facilitates this process by providing an arena of public debate" (Curran, 1991), then in regard to drugs, there is plenty of room for improvement.

References

Advisory Council on the Misuse of Drugs (ACMD) (1984) *Prevention*, London: HMSO.

Bean P (1974) *The social control of drugs*, London: Martin Robertson.

Bean P (1993) 'Cocaine and crack: the promotion of an epidemic', *in* Bean, P. (ed) *Cocaine and Crack: Supply and use*, London: Macmillan.

Beckett K (1994) 'Setting the public agenda: "street crime" and drug use in American politics', *Social Problems*, 41, 3, pp 425-47.

Berridge V & Edwards G (1987) *Opium and the People*, London: Yale University Press.

Cantril H (1940) *The Invasion From Mars: A study in the psychology of panic*, Princeton: Princeton University Press.

Cohen S (1972) *Folk Devils and Moral Panics: The creation of the mods and rockers*, London:

9

MacGibbon & Kee.

Coggans N, Shenan D, Henderson M & Danes J B (1991) *National evaluation of drug education in Scotland*, London: ISDD.

Coomber R, Morris C & Dunn L (2000) 'How the media do drugs: quality control and the reporting of drug issues in the UK print media', *International Journal of Drug Policy* (in press).

Curran J, Douglas A & Whannel G (1980) 'The Political Economy of the Human-Interest Story', in Smith A (ed.) *Newspapers and Democracy: International Essays on a Changing Medium*, Cambridge, Massachusetts: Massachusetts Institute of Technology Press.

Curran J (1991) 'Mass media and democracy: a reappraisal' in Curran, J. and Gurevitch, M. *Mass Media and Society*, London: Edward Arnold.

De Haes W (1987) 'Looking for effective drug education programmes: fifteen years exploration of the effects of different drug education programmes', *Health Education Research*, 2. 4, pp 433–38.

Edelman M (1988) *Constructing The Political Spectacle,* Chicago: University of Chicago Press.

Glover D (1984) *The Sociology of the Mass Media,* Lancs: Causeway Books.

Goode E and Ben-Yehuda N (1994) *Moral Panics: The construction of deviance,* Cambridge, Massachusetts: Blackwell.

Gossop M(1993) *Living With Drugs*, 3rd Edition, Aldershot: Ashgate.

Katz E & Lazarsfeld P (1955) *Personal Influence*, New York: The Free Press.

Kohn M (1987) *Narcomania: On heroin,* London: Faber and Faber.

Kohn M (1992) *Dope Girls: The birth of the British underground*, London: Lawrence & Wishart.

Lane D (1990) *Soviet Society Under Perestroika*, London: Unwin Hyman.

McLeod J M, Kosicki G M & Pan Z (1992) 'On Understanding and Misunderstanding Media Effects', *in* Curran, J and Gurevitch, M *Mass Media and Society*, Edward Arnold, Guildford.

Messner M A (1993) 'Outside the frame: newspaper coverage of the Sugar Ray Leonard wife abuse story', *Sociology of Sport*, 10, 2, June, pp 119–34.

Morley D (1980) *The 'Nationwide' Audience,* London: British Film Institute.

Musto D (1987) *The American Disease: Origins of narcotic control,* 2nd edition, Oxford: Oxford University Press.

Parssinen T M (1983) *Secret Passions, Secret Remedies: Narcotic drugs in British society* 1820-1930, Manchester: Manchester University Press.

Reinerman C & Levine H G (1989) 'The crack attack: politics and media in America's latest drug scare', in Best, J. (ed) *Images of Issues*, Aldine Press.

Reeves J L & Campbell R (1994) *Cracked Coverage: Television news, the anti-cocaine crusade, and the Reagan legacy,* Durham: Duke University Press.

Schaps E, DiBartolo R, Moskowitz J, Palley C S & Churgin S (1981) 'A review of 127 drug abuse prevention programme evaluations', *Journal of Drug Issues,* pp 17–43.

Shapiro H (1981) 'Press review July 1980 – May 1981', *DrugLink*, Summer 1981, ISDD.

Trebach A S (1987) *The Great Drug War: And radical proposals which could make America safe again*, New York: Macmillan.

Tichenor P J, Donohue G A & Olien C N (1970) 'Mass media flow and differential growth in knowledge', *Public Opinion Quarterly*, 34, pp 159-70.

Wisotsky S (1991) 'Not thinking like a lawyer: the case of drugs in the courts', in *Notre Dame Journal of Law, Ethic and Public Policy.* 5 (3).

drug 10 myths

TEXT | **ROSS COOMBER**

YOUR | QUESTIONS | **ANSWERED**

What are the differences between hard and soft drugs? | Do soft drugs lead to hard

drugs? | Who is pushing drugs at the school gate? | Is addiction inevitable? | Is

withdrawal that bad? | Are drugs adulterated? | What is in street drugs?

10

A myth is a popular belief which has limited use as a way of understanding the subject on which it is focused. While there are often elements of truth in all myths, in the main it could be said that they are based on stereotypical and simplistic images, which have their roots in ignorance and attribute particular characteristics to things and people that are neither supported nor substantiated by much more than hearsay. Furthermore, there are more often than not consequences (some good, some bad) for those they focus on.

Drug myths fit this description quite well. If drug users are classified as degenerate rather than in need of help they will be treated in ways appropriate to degenerates. They may be subject to harsh criminal laws instead of liberal ones; they may be feared and castigated by their friends, neighbours and community instead of accepted or supported; they may be scapegoated because of what they do and who they are. In short, by 'demonising' the drugs, invariably the same happens to those people who use them.

There are many myths about drugs. Some, like 'once an addict always an addict', have been covered elsewhere. Below, we outline a few of the hardier myths about the misuse of drugs.

What are the differences between hard and soft drugs?

The terms hard and 'soft' suggest the inherent dangers of using a particular drug. A hard drug is associated with a variety of potential dangers ranging from helpless addiction to mindless violence. Heroin and cocaine are considered to be hard drugs.

Drugs such as cannabis, ecstasy, and amphetamines are generally considered to be soft drugs because the effects are considered to be comparatively less intoxicating, less likely to lead to addiction and less likely to be dangerous for the user in general. Sounds simple enough, doesn't it? And that's the problem – not only is it too simple a way of categorising drugs, but in the light of some basic information about the drug scene as a whole, it does not stand up to much scrutiny.

Extrapolating the 'hard/soft' argument, legal drugs such as alcohol and tobacco and drugs such as paracetamol which are available in any corner shop, must be softer than the 'softest' illicit drug, otherwise they wouldn't be so widely available. Yet the dangers of misusing these drugs are well documented. Paracetamol is an effective painkiller, but in 1997 over 1,900 people died from paracetamol-related deaths (see page 61). The prescribing of over-the-counter tranquillisers often results in unwanted side effects and may lead to some form of dependence in over a third of prescribing cases (Gabe and Williams, 1986). Research has suggested that significant numbers of hospital prescriptions result in a "*major* toxic reaction" to the medicine prescribed (Gossop, 1993, p 49).

Tobacco alone is believed to be responsible for 110,000 premature deaths in Britain annually (Health Education Authority, 1991), as well as significantly contributing to thousands of cases of heart disease, thrombosis and cancer. Alcohol is considered to cause between 5,000 and 25,000 premature deaths a year and like tobacco is associated with serious health problems for many thousands more. Using the rationale of hard/soft drugs outlined at the beginning, these drugs would have to be designated as hard yet the hard/soft distinction is never applied to them in the general debate about drugs.

Risk of death is one of the benchmarks by which we label a drug as dangerous, but the number of deaths attributed to *illicit* drugs is far less than commonly thought. Even allowing for the fact that there are far fewer users of heroin than alcohol or tobacco, a smaller proportion of heroin users are likely to die from their drug of choice than smokers and drinkers. Granted, there is a far greater risk of overdosing on heroin than alcohol, and dependence is likely to take hold far more quickly than alcohol or tobacco. However, in terms of toxicity, heroin, unlike alcohol or tobacco, does not damage major organs of the body such as the heart, liver or brain and tolerance to huge doses can be built up where even decades of use result in no discernible physical damage from the drug itself. (A regular and reliable supply of heroin may be taken with relatively little impact on the user. It is when supply is interrupted that problems are likely to be encountered.) The main dangers (dependence or overdose apart) relate to *how* the drug is taken. Thus the use of dirty or contaminated needles presents dangers as great as the drug itself.

The historical and cultural context in which drug use takes place also influences the hard/soft distinction. There was a time in the 1960s and '70s in the USA, for example, when cocaine was viewed as a relatively benign drug which caused few problems. The advent of crack radically changed this perspective.

By contrast cannabis in the 1950s was associated with numerous harmful attributes, including powerful addictive properties, violence-inducing tendencies and the likelihood of producing both moral and physical degeneration. Today, these views have very little credibility. Undoubtedly cannabis would have been considered a hard drug in the 1950s whereas in the 1990s it is generally seen as a 'soft' one.

Another problem with the oppositional separation into hard and soft, is that it may conjure up an image of soft drugs as harmless. All drugs have some level of danger attached to their use. Ecstasy use has been associated with a number of deaths in recent years (ISDD, 1999) mainly related to heatstroke when combined with long periods of intense dancing. Amphetamine use can lead to a range of problems (tiredness, delusions, paranoia, psychosis, addiction) depending on the regularity and severity of use. Amphetamine is considered a soft drug yet its effects are similar to those of cocaine. Cannabis smoke appears to be more damaging than cigarette smoke in relation to respiratory complaints and diseases, while an inexperienced LSD user may suffer distressing psychological effects from the trip. Solvents, barely considered in the ambit of soft drugs, in reality kill substantially more young people in the 12-19 age group than all the other substances put together (Taylor *et al*, 1994; Home Office Statistical Bulletin, 1993).

Finally, the categorisation of drugs into soft and hard is often a reflection of what is also a politically expedient approach to understanding drugs. Historically, groups lobbying for the legalisation or the decriminalisation of cannabis have sought to distinguish the drug from harder ones by claiming cannabis to be a drug

10

10

with few attendant problems compared to the severity of harm caused by drugs like heroin. Similarly, the anti-drug lobby constructs an image of illicit drugs whereby soft drugs are shown to be no better than hard drugs because they seduce the user to seek the stronger, more intense experiences promised by their more dangerous relatives.

Do soft drugs lead to hard drugs?

Another reason why certain illicit drugs are sometimes referred to as soft and hard relates to the long-held belief that experimentation with or regular use of certain drugs (particularly cannabis) will lead – as sure as night follows day – to the use of harder drugs. The theory goes that the user is exposed to drugtaking, is seduced by its pleasures and moves on to bigger and better things. It is in this way that drugs such as cannabis and amphetamines are seen as being gateway or stepping-stone drugs. However, the relationship and transition between different drugs is not quite as simple as this.

While studies consistently show that nearly all heroin addicts have used cannabis it is also clear that only a small minority of cannabis users will move on to hard drug use. If this were not true, then there would be many more heroin users given the millions who have ever tried cannabis (perhaps eight million people in Britain alone). A recent government survey found that although 96 per cent of people who'd used opiates in the past year had also taken cannabis, only 7 per cent of cannabis users had taken opiates (Leitner *et al*, 1993 p 203). There is as much of a causal link between cannabis use and heroin use as there is between a kid drinking shandy and a tramp drinking meths – they may be at opposite ends of a spectrum but that doesn't mean there's a clear progression from one to the other.

Although it is true that cannabis use is the most common first *illegal* drug to be used, most cannabis users have already experimented with tobacco and alcohol, both of which have significant psychoactive and physiological effects. In fact, many heavy cannabis users never try drugs such as heroin, and often exhibit the same negative prejudices and accept some of the stereotypes about heroin users as members of the non drug-using population.

Gossop (1993, p 103) makes the point that ironically the number of cannabis users who experiment with other drugs may be swollen by the simple fact that in order to get hold of cannabis, users have to mix with dealers who may supply other drugs and are tempted to experiment with them much more than if the current controls on cannabis did not make this association necessary.

That said, there clearly are cannabis users who do move on to heroin. There are also social drinkers who go on to become alcoholics (and, come to think of it, people who learn sport at school who go on to win Olympic medals). The point however is that there is nothing inevitable about this progression. There is nothing inherent in cannabis, or a glass of wine, or a run round a football field which propels people up (or down) an inevitable slope.

Who is pushing drugs at the school gate?

One of the most common and hardy drug myths is that of the evil pusher at the school gates or some other opportunist place (the ice cream van is another favourite) enticing vulnerable young children into drug use in order to increase their sales. There is little, if indeed any, evidence to support such a view. In reality, there are a number of amalgamated myths that help construct this particular picture. One such long-standing myth is the idea that the dealer will provide free samples in order to hook the child, and that once hooked the child will bring a new and regular income. There are a couple of problems with this scenario:

- Most schoolchildren do not have a regular and sufficient income to actually become dependent on drugs, which can be a lengthy and expensive process.
- Pushing drugs onto schoolchildren would also present an unreasonable risk to the seller. Parents and teachers would soon learn of such a character and act accordingly.

Although there is little research on drug dealing in schools, it is likely that where drugs are available in school, it will be one of the students who has access to them and is either dealing to make a bit of cash or selling their own excess to friends.

There has always been a fear of the unscrupulous and degenerate character preying on the weakest for their own gain. The fact that the archetypal pusher is not found or caught rarely disproves to believers that he did not exist in the first place. Unfortunately for the mythmakers, initial and early drug use has little to do with pushers as they are conventionally portrayed. Initial provision of an illicit drug is nearly always from within the peer group (friends and acquaintances) or the family (an older brother or sister). It is unlikely that unknown pushers would have much success enticing people into drug use as they are not equipped with the security of the peer/kin group, which gives the drug credibility and desirability, and provide a setting in which it can be taken and learned about, thereby providing a context in which second, third and continuing use can occur.

This persistent mythology sets up parents and children to resist temptation from evil strangers, but this can divert attention from the settings where experimentation is most likely to occur. Friends, friends of friends, relatives and neighbours are not drug fiends, but they are more likely to be the source of drug experimentation than a menacing figure in shadow and shades.

Is addiction inevitable?

The notion that certain drugs have the power to make individuals immediately crave them and compel them towards more use and inevitable addiction is yet another drug fallacy. Recently we have heard much about the powers of crack cocaine to produce instant addiction. This is not the first time a drug has been given such a press. Heroin is another drug to which such powers are often attributed: an American book was titled *It's So Good Don't Even Try it Once*.

In reality, the process of becoming dependent on heroin, for example, is quite

10

10

lengthy and relies on a number of factors related to personal circumstances. Most people who try it for the first time are physically sick and won't bother again. Others will try it a few times and then decide heroin isn't for them. If you carry on taking the drug, tolerance builds up so that you need higher and more frequent doses to get the same effect. If you got to the point where you were using the drug on a daily basis and then suddenly stopped using it, you would experience the classic heroin withdrawal symptoms. This would mean your body had become physically dependent on heroin and you feel ill if you stop using. To feel normal you would need to take more heroin. Even then, it can take several months for somebody to reach the point where they are so hooked on heroin both physically and psychologically that it completely dominates their life (Kaplan, 1983).

The effects of smoking crack cocaine are very different to smoking or injecting heroin, but many of the lessons are the same. Dependence on any drug does not occur solely because of the drug's effects. Although crack cocaine provides a quick and intense euphoria and dependence *may* occur more quickly than to cocaine powder, to become addicted to crack (a psychological addiction in this case) an individual has to be 'dedicated' to the daily ritual of obtaining money for drugs, arranging to buy them, use them, come down from the effects and start all over again. 'Crack' is one of the more recent drugs to be labelled 'instantly addictive', but there is enough research evidence to show that many people do not enjoy the crack experience and fail to repeat it, while others can 'take it or leave it', primarily because to acquire a 'crack habit' means finding hundreds of pounds every week (Ditton and Hammersley, 1994; Miller, 1991; Newcombe, 1989). The association with instant addiction and this particular drug may say more about the type of user *most visible* in the US experience. Research into freebase cocaine users and some crack users suggests that many are in fact more heavily involved in heavy and multiple drug use than other users. Thus the scare over the powers of crack may have been exacerbated by the *visibility* of existing heavy drug users using a new drug (crack) to excess and apparently demonstrating its ability to hook quickly and easily those people already heavily involved in a drug-using lifestyle.

Is withdrawal that bad?

A common myth about heroin dependence is that the pain of withdrawal is unbearable and even life-threatening. This is probably a major reason why many heroin users are scared of giving up the drug and it also helps reinforce the notion that heroin is a drug which enslaves users for ever, or at least until they die. Abrupt withdrawal from some drugs such as alcohol, barbiturates and tranquillisers can be highly dangerous, but for many users the effects of withdrawing from heroin are similar to a very bad dose of flu – not very pleasant, but hardly life-threatening.

Of course physically withdrawing from the drug so that it is no longer in the body, is only the beginning of the process of coming off drugs. As one musician said many years ago about heroin, "they can get it out of your body, but they can't get it out of your mind". Although this is an exaggeration, it is true that rehabilitation is a long process involving major changes of attitude, motivation, lifestyle and so on, so that drugs are no longer the central feature of a person's life.

Are drugs adulterated?

There is a widespread notion that dangerous adulteration adds considerably to the risks of illicit drug use. It's often implied that users play a kind of pharmacological Russian roulette. In fact the risks from dangerous cutting agents (see below) are negligible.

It is commonly believed by the general public, accepted by drug users and health professionals, and reported by the media, that street drugs such as heroin are adulterated (cut) with dangerous substances (cutting agents): brick dust, rat-poison, ground up light bulb glass, chalk and scouring powders such as Vim and Ajax among others (Coomber, 1997a 1997b, and 1999a). Actual examination of drugs indicates that far less cutting takes place than is generally thought to be the case (Coomber, 1997c, 1999b).

With heroin, what cutting does take place is predominantly carried out before importation and with substances that often enhance, not diminish the drug's effect. Adulteration is by and large not due to the haphazard desperation of a 'strung-out junkie', or the routine dilution of the drug as it makes its way through the chain of distribution.

What is in street drugs?

Forensic analysis of street drugs does not find any of the substances listed above. In heroin the most common cutting agents in the late 1990s are caffeine and paracetamol. Comprehensive analysis of heroin samples by the US Drug Enforcement Administration (DEA) since 1990 reveals numerous sugars, prescription drugs (primarily paracetamol), opium alkaloids and occasionally salts. None of the dangerous cutting agents commonly claimed and feared have been found. In Europe, sugars are less likely to be found in heroin. But, here as well, dangerous cutting agents are not found.

One recent survey of heroin street seizures from around the UK found that nearly 50 per cent of the 228 samples tested did not contain any adulterants at all. This indicates that the cutting of street drugs is far from a predictable outcome of passing through the chain of distribution. Analysis of US heroin (from Mexico) found that in some major cities, even where the selling is gang controlled, buying adulterated heroin may be difficult.

There are a number of reasons why less cutting takes place than is normally assumed (Coomber, 1997d). Dealers usually resort to safer methods of increasing profit from drug sales, such as selling smaller amounts for proportionately more. A related method is selling short measures. A dealer may make 30 single gram wraps from an ounce instead of the standard 28 (Coomber, 1997b, 1997d). These

10

10

methods result in additional profit but do not contaminate the sample (which they usually assume has already been cut). There is no additional danger beyond that entailed in the drug itself.

Risk in drug selling is perceived as a two-way street. Dealers fear reprisal if they were thought to be selling bad drugs. Also, it is not unusual for them to want to protect a reputation for selling good quality drugs. There is also a reasonable concern that they do not want to harm others (Coomber, 1997b, 1997d). Drug dealers are generally not chemists or otherwise knowledgeable about what is a healthy or dangerous cutting substance. The result is that the cutting of street drugs by dealers or desperate addicts is neither systematic nor predictable.

Why is cutting presumed?

Given there is almost no forensic evidence to suggest that dangerous cutting agents are put into street drugs, why is the belief in it so strong? Even drug dealers believe that other dealers do it.

The question is worth asking because there seems to be little concrete evidence to support the notion, even from drug users. The residue left after preparing injected and/or inhaled drugs shows no evidence of unusual insoluble cutting agents, or other indications of adulteration with dangerous substances (Coomber, unpublished)

If adulterants are not found in the residue, then where? Users often believe they can tell when a drug they have taken contains something other than the primary drug. In one research sample, 37 of 319 previously taken ecstasy samples were believed by those users to have contained heroin (Forsyth, 1995). Heroin has never been found in ecstasy.

In another sample, cocaine users provided the researcher with cocaine they believed to be adulterated with amphetamine: something they and many others believed to be a common cutting agent of cocaine. No amphetamine was found in these samples and forensic analysis almost never finds amphetamine in cocaine (Cohen, 1989).

Is LSD often contaminated with strychnine?

LSD users often believe the stomach ache that sometimes accompanies use of this drug comes from strychnine in the original solution. One user told me this was well known. Strychnine is not found in LSD.

When a user has an adverse reaction to a drug it is not uncommon to blame dangerous cutting agents. This line of thought is particularly evident among peers when the individual concerned is an experienced user. It is also the first line of thought for authorities such as the police when responding to a tragedy like the death of Leah Betts. Analysis of Leah Betts' ecstasy did not reveal anything but the pure drug. To my knowledge this is always the case in these circumstances.

Adverse reactions

In cases of overdose and other adverse reactions to drugs such as heroin, where samples are analysed nothing unusual is generally found. Purity can sometimes be very high, but this is also not common. Blood tests of those who end up in hospital do not show poisons other than the drug in question.

More reasoned explanations of why adverse reactions occur relate to build-up overdose. The individual consumes more than normal over a period of time, without realising it. This also partly explains why such events can happen to only one user in a group, where all had been using the same sample.

A usual factor in adverse reactions is drug mixing, most commonly with alcohol. One recent research paper suggested that most events recorded as heroin overdoses are in fact nothing of the sort (Darke and Zador, 1996).

A third contributing factor to adverse reactions is inappropriate co-activity. With ecstasy this would be over-exertion without periodic re-hydration or chilling-out, or over re-hydration – drinking too much water.

Belief without evidence

If users cannot in reality tell whether a drug is cut with particular substances or not and do not find suspicious residue in their drugs post-preparation, why do they assume dangerous cutting practices are to blame for ill-health or overdose? It is difficult to know exactly how a belief system such as this arises in the absence of concrete evidence. It is almost unquestioned and believed even by those who are supposed to do it – the dealers. There are three primary issues

- the development of images of the dope-fiend at the end of the last century and up to the present day
- certain common drug myths re-enforce each other, each proving the truth of the other
- the clandestine nature of drug supply (Coomber, 1997e).

Drugs like heroin and cocaine have long had the reputation of transforming users into moral degenerates. Over 50 years ago the dope fiend was associated with the capability to carry out the most heinous of crimes. '... [he] becomes a moral degenerate, liar, thief, etc, because of the direct influence of the drug' (Lindesmith, 1941).

The heroin campaigns of the 1980s presented similar images of moral degeneracy brought about by addiction (Rhodes, 1990). Media images of pushers at school gates and street corners targeting the young, depict drug dealers as willing to hook the most vulnerable members of society to ensure a steady custom.

Drug transformation

The supposed transformative powers of drugs are important to understanding how dangerous adulteration could be believed. Knowingly putting dangerous substances, such as strychnine, ground glass or scouring powders, into drugs that you are to sell is clearly an act of pre-meditated violence or of diminished responsibility. Both fit into the broad spectrum of beliefs about how this practice occurs, but neither makes any real sense.

10

10

Even the strung-out junkie who doesn't care what they put into the drugs they sell in order to dilute them (diminished responsibility/morally degenerate), would find it is easier to grab sugar off the shelf, or buy glucose or lactose (both cheap) than to find strychnine, or spend time grinding down a brick or a light-bulb, or chalk.

A number of drug myths, when considered in isolation, do not hold up to scrutiny. There is little or no evidence for the pusher at the street corner/school gate preying on children and giving away free samples. Such pushers are not found, though stories of them are common, and drugs like heroin do not become addictive quickly enough to make this a viable economic activity (Kaplan, 1983). When combined with the assumption of dangerous adulteration they gain plausibility. Thus, the evil drug dealer, likely to prey on the young becomes credible because of the widely accepted existence of dangerous drug adulteration.

The chain of assumption runs: dangerous drug adulteration occurs because the transformative powers of drugs degenerate the moral faculties of drug dealers (turns them into dope fiends and junkies) and make it possible or, in times of desperation, likely. Of course, only crazy or evil individuals would cut the drugs they sell with dangerous substances and to such individuals, pushing drugs on the vulnerable would give little concern.

But dangerous drug adulteration does not occur. Rather than showing no regard for their customers, dealers are often concerned not to harm them (Coomber, 1997b). A more considered view of who and what the drug dealer is must be the outcome. Without the underlying assumptions relating to dangerous adulteration, other drug myths are left with little or no foundation.

Buyer beware

To these concerns must be added the context in which drug selling takes place. Mistrust of retailers by consumers is common even in licit buying and selling. A second-hand car may have been patched-up, written-off or stolen. The 'pure' orange juice or the '100 per cent beef' product we buy may be something quite different. Concern about being cheated or ripped-off is part of everyday life, so we should not be surprised when such fears and anxieties are magnified in an illicit and clandestine market.

To some extent consumers of drugs may even invest in the danger of the illicit market place. Drug use is generally a fairly mundane activity. Convincing yourself that there is a possible danger in every hit, beyond that of the drug, arguably makes it a little bit more interesting.

Common assumptions about dangerous drug adulteration are, by and large, mistaken. Dangerous cutting agents do not represent significant risk to drug users. Drugs are not cut with any substance routinely or haphazardly down through the chain of distribution.

In fact the contaminants found in heroin for smoking, such as caffeine or paracetamol, often increase the amount of heroin available rather than reducing the quality of the drug.

By emphasising imaginary risks of dangerous cutting agents, the media and other authorities divert attention from the real risks of the drugs and the inappropriate activities that may accompany their use. They also reproduce unhelpful stereotypes about drugs, addiction and those who sell drugs.

References

Cohen P (1989) *Cocaine Use in Amsterdam – in Non-Deviant Sub-Cultures*, Amsterdam: University of Amsterdam Press.

Coomber R (1997a), 'Vim in the veins – fantasy or fact: the adulteration of illicit drugs', *Addiction Research*, 5(3), p 195-212.

Coomber R (1997b) 'The adulteration of drugs: what dealers do, what dealers do, what dealers think', *Addiction Research* 5(4), p 297-306.

Coomber R (1997c), 'How often does the adulteration/dilution of heroin actually occur: an analysis of 228 street samples across the UK (1995-1996) and discussion of monitoring policy', *International Journal of Drug Policy*, 8(4), p 178-186.

Coomber R (1997d) 'Dangerous drug adulteration – an international survey of drug dealers using the internet and the world wide web (www)', *International Journal of Drug Policy*, 8(2), p 18-28.

Coomber R (1997e) 'Adulteration of drugs: the discovery of a myth', *Contemporary Drug Problems*: 24(2), p 239-71.

Coomber R (1999a) 'Lay perceptions and beliefs about the adulteration of illicit drugs in 1990s: a student sample', *Addiction Research* 7(4) p 323-38.

Coomber R (1999b) 'The cutting of heroin in the United States in the 1990s', *Journal of Drug Issues*.

Coomber R 'Post-preparation residue: a contribution to beliefs in the dangerous adulteration of street drugs?' Unpublished research.

Darke S & Zador D (1996) 'Fatal heroin overdose: a review', *Addiction*, 91(12), p 1765-72.

Ditton J & Hammersley R (1994) 'The typical cocaine user', *DrugLink*, November/December, ISDD.

Forsyth A J M (1995) 'Ecstasy and illegal drug design: a new concept in drug use', *International Journal of Drug Policy*, 6(3). p 193-209.

Gabe J & Williams P (eds.) (1986) *Tranquillisers: Social, Psychological and Clinical Perspectives*, Tavistock, London.

Gossop M (1993) *Living with Drugs* (3rd edition), Arena, Cambridge.

Health Education Authority (1991) *The smoking epidemic: counting the cost in England*, HEA, London.

Home Office Statistical Bulletin (1993) *Statistics of drug addicts notified to the Home Office, United Kingdom 1992*. Issue 15/93, 27 May.

ISDD (1999) *UK Drug Situation: 1999. A report by ISDD*. London: ISDD.

Kaplan J (1983) *The Hardest Drug: Heroin and public policy*, Chicago: University of Chicago Press.

Leitner M *et al* (1993) *Drug usage and drugs prevention*, HMSO, London.

Lindesmith A R (1941) 'Dope fiend mythology', *Journal of Criminal Law and Criminology*: 32, p 199-208.

10

10

Miller R M (1991) *The Case for Legalising Drugs*, Westport: Praeger

Newcombe R & Matthews L (1989) 'Crack in Liverpool', *DrugLink*, September/October, p16.

Newcombe R (1994) *Ecstasy Deaths and Other Fatalities Related to Dance Drugs and Raving*, Information Document 4, Liverpool: 3D Research Bureau.

Rhodes T (1990) 'The politics of anti-drugs campaigns', *DrugLink* 5(3), p 16-18.

Taylor J C, Norman C L, Bland J M, Anderson H R & Ramsey J D (1994) *Trends in deaths associated with abuse of volatile substances* 1971-1992, Report No 7, St George's Hospital Medical School, London.

11

what is drug testing?

TEXT | **GARY HAYES**

11

Introduction
Although drug testing has been around for a while, particularly police testing of drivers, it is only since the 1980s that testing has seen an expansion into many sectors. This chapter looks at what drug testing is, where it is carried out and why.

What is drug testing?
Drug testing is a way of detecting the presence of drugs in a person's body. Testing can detect most drugs, although there appears to be no simple screening test for hallucinogens such as LSD and magic mushrooms. On the whole, tests are available for alcohol, heroin, amphetamine, cannabis, barbiturates, benzodiazepines (Valium, etc), cocaine, methadone and for a number of performance-enhancing drugs.

There are various ways of testing for the presence of drugs. The method used depends on why testing is needed, the expected outcome of testing, and who is being tested. The different testing methods test different parts of the body. Some are more intrusive than others, meaning they may or may not puncture the skin.

How are people tested?
Self-report questionnaires
Questionnaires are used primarily as a screening tool. They are non-intrusive, easy to administer and inexpensive. As with all questionnaires, however, there is no way of guaranteeing that respondents will tell the truth, particularly if the consequences of doing so are not in their own interests.

Sweat
The police have shown repeated interest in the use of a roadside test that uses swabs to collect sweat from the face or forehead. Although it has been tested on several occasions, none are currently being used in this way. Sweat tests are used in the US to monitor parolees and prisoners. The sweat patches used are usually worn like a bandage , and are made tamper proof (ie, attempts at removal can be seen). After being worn for several days, the patches are placed in a protective container and sent to a laboratory for analysis. In the case of drugs such as cocaine, heroin and cannabis, sweat tests can prove as accurate as urine tests. They can provide a cumulative measure of use and therefore may be used to assess how much an individual has used a particular drug.

Saliva
These tests are often sold as commercial devices under names such as Salivette, Orasure and Epitope. Saliva collection is relatively unintrusive and can be administered by non-medical personnel in informal settings. Adulteration of samples is difficult, although because of the very small amounts of drug residue found in saliva, they may fail to pick up traces of some drugs. In some cases contaminations

from drug residues found in the oral and nasal cavity may give false positive (showing wrongly that an illegal drug has been taken) results. Saliva tests can also be used to test for alcohol in the body.

Breath

Breath testing is the most commonly used test for alcohol. Like a urine test, a breath test is non-invasive (ie, sample taking does not involve a medical procedure). It is also cheap, and the result is virtually instantaneous.

Urine

Urine testing is the most popular form of test because it is easy to get a sample, and quick and relatively cheap to get a result. A sample is taken, often under supervision to prevent cheating or adulteration, and submitted for analysis either using an on-site test or a laboratory. Strict collection and analysis protocols, known as chain-of-custody procedures, help to prevent contamination or mixing of samples, but, as shown in prisons, adulteration is not uncommon. Whereas urine testing in a laboratory can produce 100 per cent accuracy, on-site tests are generally unreliable.

Laboratories use a combination of two analytical techniques, gas chromatography and mass spectrometry. The first physically separates the various substances that have been extracted from the specimen. The second identifies specific substances separated by the gas chromatography using the unique colour spectrum refracted by each of the drugs (residue or secondary drugs found in body as a result of the primary drug's use) to identify the exact molecule or metabolite.

Quick and convenient on-site tests can test a sample almost immediately, using test sticks and colour or pattern charts to identify the presence of a drug in the body. Some devices identify one drug, others identify several. As only an indicator of a drug's presence, these easy tests are recommended only as screening devices. Positive samples are normally sent for further analysis to confirm results using the techniques described above.

Hair and nails

The testing of people's hair is increasing in popularity. The police, for example, now hair-test prospective recruits coming into the force. Testing hair, although relatively expensive (nearly twice that of urine tests), is non-invasive. Because a hair is the result of months of growth, testing can reveal a history of drug use, going back months or even years. (Alcohol, however, cannot be tested in this way.) Any hair on the body can be tested. One doctor in the US for example showed that Keats used opium by finding traces of it in strands of his hair. Unless an individual shaves off all her/his hair, this test is said to be virtually evasion proof. Nails can be tested in the same way.

Samples are usually taken from near the scalp at the crown of the head, removing the root and tip of the hair. Hair testing is considered by many as one of the least accurate tests, mainly because hair can be contaminated by sweat or from the

11

environment (through smoke or powder). There is no established measure for dose or time of use.

Concern has also been raised at the possibility of the test being ethnically biased because of the difference in hair types and levels of melanin (a chemical which can affect drug retention in hair). People with dark skin and hair, for example, tend to retain more cocaine and amphetamines than people with white skin and fair hair. There is also a question as to the relevance of testing for drug use many weeks or months before the time of screening.

Blood

Testing someone's blood requires medical skill. It is therefore expensive as well as invasive – ie, it requires puncturing the skin. Blood tests are only usually carried out in circumstances where a complex and accurate analysis is required, such as after a road or rail accident. Detection times are shorter for blood than for urine or hair tests. Blood tests can estimate the time of use of cannabis and some prescription drugs by using concentration levels of certain cannabis metabolites in the blood plasma, but these tend to be unreliable.

Why are tests used?

Tests are mainly used:

- as a tool for monitoring and screening an employee's ability and perceived suitability for work
- for monitoring drug use among those in and entering the criminal justice system
- for those following a treatment regime
- screening for illicit and performance-enhancing drugs in sport.

Drug testing employees

Drug testing employees is on the increase in the UK. An estimated 10 per cent of employers screen at recruitment for drugs and 5 per cent test randomly, and this is expected to rise sharply in the coming decade. In the USA, 81 per cent of large companies currently test.

The prison service has indicated that it intends to test all CARATS workers (see Chapter 8) on recruitment and randomly during service, a practice the police currently carry out. Several public schools have also said they might begin testing pupils and possibly teachers (some international schools already test teachers), on the grounds that drug taking is an unacceptable activity in or out of school.

Drug and alcohol testing is a very effective way of addressing employee drug and alcohol use, particularly in safety-sensitive situations. Testing is, therefore, prevalent in the transport and oil industries and on the increase in the manufacturing sector, where machinery is operated. Other sectors, such as finance, have introduced pre-employment testing even where there is no risk to public safety, on the grounds that there should be no risk to profitability or productivity either.

What are the main uses of drug testing in employment?

Recruitment screening

Some employers test all job applicants for drug use. Notification is given of the test, and those found positive are deselected. Testing at this stage sends a clear message about company attitude, and deters possible problematic users from seeking employment (as well as others who are not problematic users). The main assumption made by those who test at this stage is that drug users tend to perform less well than non-users. Recruitment screening is used by the police and the military to de-select potential recruits.

Random testing

Random testing has proved useful in detecting use of drugs by those in safety-sensitive positions or when a significant drug or alcohol problem is thought to exist. Testing in the UK outside these situations is uncommon, although London Underground tests all staff regardless of where they work.

Routine testing

Employees are informed in advance of a forthcoming drug test. Although routine tests are not designed to catch people out, they act as a deterrent to drug use. Routine testing may also form part of an employee's treatment plan agreed by the employer. In circumstances where safety is not an issue, such tests may prove overly expensive and intrusive.

Cause detection

This method is often used following accidents involving transport or machinery. The use of such tests as standard practice acts as a useful deterrent, and following an incident is useful in confronting an employee's denial.

Alternative testing

Criticism of drug tests has led to some support for impairment-based screening, such as hand-eye coordination tests, which would appear to provide the most direct measure of intoxication. These tests are non-invasive and appraise the issue of work safety directly by addressing the employee's performance rather than past drug use, which may or may not affect actual workplace safety. Such tests address ethical issues in relation to civil liberties and employment associated with drug and alcohol testing. The police are currently looking at adopting procedures for roadside testing in light of the drawbacks of the other tests (such as accuracy and inability to distinguish a level of present intoxication).

Drug testing in the criminal justice system

Mandatory drug testing

Mandatory drug testing (MDT) is carried out systematically and randomly as part of the government's drive to prevent drug use in prisons. Administered in every

11

UK prison and young offender institute, the tests, as the name suggests, are obligatory. Refusal to take a test often results in action against the prisoner, such as removal of privileges.

Urine samples of inmates are taken either randomly or as part of a routine testing (and treatment) regime. Concern has been raised at the effect repeated testing is having on the drug-taking behaviour of inmates. As drugs like cannabis often remain in the body for up to four weeks, prisoners are thought to be switching from cannabis to heroin – which only remains for up to three days in the body.

Since its introduction, MDT has shown a large drop in positive results, from 33 per cent in 1995/96 to just over 18 per cent in 1999. That trend, in addition to indicating that MDT is a deterrent to drug use, may also indicate the sophistication with which prisoners are able to avoid detection. Methods range from contaminating urine samples with soap hidden under the nails to timing drug use or changing drug types to fit in with estimated testing times.

Drug Treatment and Testing Orders (DTTOs)

In an attempt to break the apparent link between drug use and crime, the government has introduced the option of taking treatment as a community sentence using DTTOs. A key component of the orders is the regular testing of participants to monitor their progress in reducing or stopping the taking of drugs. Refusal to take a test or a positive result can result in the order being reviewed and a custodial sentence being applied.

Drug testing arrestees

The government also proposes to introduce mandatory testing for arrestees suspected of committing 'trigger offences' (ie, acquisitive crime) or for drugs offences. Refusal to be tested, regardless of whether an arrestee has been convicted, may, under the proposals, result in detention. Non-obligatory testing already takes place in a number of prisons in England as part of the NEW-ADAM project to monitor the incidence of drug use among arrestees (see Chapter 5a).

Drug testing in treatment

Mostly urine, but also blood, testing can be helpful in monitoring and promoting abstinence and can be seen as a motivator for participants to stay clean. Some rehabilitation centres require clients to be drug free before entry, and therefore screen potential clients. Treatment testing is often routine, creating set goals for the client to reach abstention and then maintain it. In some circumstances, random testing is used to check on the using-status of a client, but this method can prove intrusive and create an atmosphere of mistrust.

Drug testing in sport

Drug testing takes place at the higher levels of competitive sport. Competitors are tested not only for performance-enhancing drugs (such as steroids) but also for illicit drugs, such as cannabis. Urine testing looks for the presence of a steroid or one or more of its unique metabolites. The International Olympic Committee issues a list of banned substances, which are tested for at competitions and during training periods. It is up to athletes to ensure that these drugs are not contained in any medicine or foods.

How long do drugs stay in the body?

The length of time that any drug stays in the body varies and can depend on food and fluid intake, metabolic rate, kidney function, amount of drug taken and for how long, how it was taken, whether other drugs were taken with it and the sensitivity of the test – see table below.

London Underground, for example, advise staff that to guarantee starting work with near zero alcohol levels in the body, no more than seven units should be taken in the previous 24 hours (eg, about three pints) and none in the previous eight hours.

Table 11.1 | **Drug detection periods**
A rough guide to how long different drugs can be detected in urine after use at dose levels typically taken by drug users.

Cannabis	
casual use	2-7 days
heavy use	up to 30 days
Amphetamine	2-4 days
Ecstasy	2-4 days
Diazepam	1-2 days
Temazepam	1-2 days
Alcohol	12-24 hours
Heroin	1-2 days (longer after IV* use)
Buprenorphine	2-3 days (longer after IV use)
Cocaine	12 hrs-3 days
Methadone	2 days
LSD	2-3 days

*IV = intraveneous use

Steroid retention varies, from a few months with nandrolone decanoate to a few days with oxandrolone.

11

11 Are tests accurate?

Urine and other tests (except for the breathalyser for alcohol) cannot show whether performance was impaired by a drug at the time of the test. A regular cannabis smoker may have to give it up if her/his employer routinely tests for drugs, as cannabis is detectable up to a month after use. There are some blood tests that can estimate how long ago some drugs, such as cannabis, were taken.

False positives (which show, wrongly, that an illegal drug has been taken) are most common when a drug group being tested for is present in small amounts in a legal product; for example, codeine in cold medicines breaks down to morphine in the liver. Most testing agencies allow for such instances, usually by informing the testee that a substance has been traced and that they should be informed of any medication or food supplements taken recently.

False positives can also happen if the testing staff are inexperienced or the equipment is contaminated.

Although not a false positive as such, passive smoking can result in traces of drugs in the system being found by testing. One such case was the Olympic snowboarding champion who, after testing positive for cannabis, appealed successfully on the grounds that his test result was caused by socialising with friends who regularly smoke the drug.

The accuracy of tests has been called into question within athletics. A number of athletes (eg, Linford Christie) have appealed the results of their positive tests on the grounds that certain food supplements have raised levels of certain restricted drugs within the body. The rationale here is that the athlete has not purposefully taken the banned drug, despite it being present in the body. Other athletes have also called into question the testing procedures, which, they say, caused contamination.

As with all tests, the presence of a drug in a sample can be attributed to many factors. Test results should therefore be open to interpretation and consequential action part of a clear and open procedure.

False negatives (giving a clear reading when in fact a drug was taken) may also occur where the drug or its metabolites is found in too small quantities, either due to rapid detoxification, using anti-detection kits, or cheating (contaminating or providing a clean sample from a friend). Quick on-site tests, particularly saliva tests, commonly give 10 per cent false negatives due to their unreliability and the low level of drug residue found in the body. For this reason, some employers who use this method send a random 10 per cent of samples for further analysis.

Deceiving the tester

There are of course ways of avoiding a positive test if a drug has been used. Specialised anti-detection kits help disguise or remove traceable drugs in the body, and are a safe and legal way to avoid unwanted detection.

There are other, less sophisticated ways of avoiding detection. One way is to purposefully contaminate the sample (of urine) using soap, detergent, or anything else that will render the sample useless. By doing this, testees buy themselves time while the sample is tested and rejected. Timing is another way some testees avoid detection. Inmates are thought to be restricting their drug use to weekends, aware of the fact that drug testing usually takes place mid-week.

Deception occurs in some sports, particularly prior to important competitions when performance-enhancing drugs can greatly increase the chance of winning. Users use as much of the drug as they can during training, then expel the drug using diuretics (ie, drugs that help cleans the kidneys and system of toxins). However, competition organisers often test for banned diuretics in the urine of athletes. Some athletes use other drugs to mask the use of steroids – eg, probenecid, a common prescription drug.

What are the safeguards for accurate testing?

To avoid inaccurate test results, the testing industry has set out the following basic recommendations.

- Chain-of-custody conditions, which mark and chart the progress of the sample from provision to end result, should provide a record of the progress of a urine specimen from collection to the reporting of the results. A specially designed kit should be used with space to record declared medication.
- Results should be interpreted by a medical review officer as no test can determine whether a drug has been used for legitimate purposes or illegally.
- The only laboratory test procedure that should be accepted in court is an initial immuno-assay screen confirmed by gas chromatography/mass spectrometry.

What is the legal situation?

Apart from public transport law (see below) there is no specific UK legislation on drug testing. Neither are there any court rulings to provide legal precedent. It is therefore impossible to know what might stand up in a court of law if tests or results are challenged.

Employment

The Transport and Works Act 1992 makes it illegal for a person to be intoxicated or under the influence of drugs while working on any kind of railway or tramway system where public safety in involved. This applies to drivers, guards, signalmen, and maintenance staff, and also to their supervisors. In a sense, this is an extension of the Road Traffic Act, which covers driving on the road while under the influence of drugs.

Nothing in law prevents an employer requiring an employee to be tested at interview or including testing in a contract of employment. Most job offers are conditional on a satisfactory medical report and this might include testing. If a recruit finds this unacceptable, all they can really do is either not go for the interview or refuse the job.

There are some reservations about more intrusive testing, such as blood testing,

11

although the legality of this is still to be tested in court.

Refusal to comply with an employer's imposition of drug testing on existing employees might be seen as disobeying a 'reasonable instruction'; the employer may be within their rights to take disciplinary action. An exception might be medically invasive tests (like blood tests), which require the employee's consent. Courts might take a dim view of an employer who suddenly announced random drug testing without prior consultations with the workforce.

Education

Nothing in law prevents a state or public school introducing drug testing of pupils, but no pupil can be tested against their will. In public schools, drug testing could be included in the contract between school and parent. If a public school pupil then refused, this might be interpreted as breach of contract and the pupil expelled (or given whatever penalty is in the contract).

Sport

Sports bodies affiliated to the Sports Council must have a testing procedure. In theory this means that Sunday league football players could be tested if their league is affiliated to the Football Association, which in turn is affiliated to the Sports Council. In practice, testing happens among the sporting elite, where legal challenges have been launched against alleged restraint of trade. At lower levels of sport there would probably be no such defence against a positive test.

Are there any drug testing guidelines?

There are no guidelines for drug testing in the UK. Most reputable laboratories follow US government guidelines. Drug testing on its own can cause more harm than the prevention it promises. Testing generally should be part of a drug and alcohol policy, which defines the need for its introduction, provides education and information, and offers advice and care if problems arise. Crucially, employees need to view drug testing as a necessary part of running an organisation. The introduction of tests should be appraised as part of the overall organisational policy. There are a number of issues however that should be considered when introducing testing:

- Is there a sufficient drug problem affecting safety and performance to warrant testing?
- What are the goals of introducing testing? Are these goals reasonable, and are they directly affected by testing?
- Will testing cause more resentment than help necessary prevention?

What are the objections to testing?

Despite its increase in apparent popularity, testing is a controversial issue. It is usually justified on the grounds that it is a measure of someone's ability to drive, fly or operate machinery. Indeed, testing in certain work settings can serve as a useful deterrent and in others, such as those covered by the 1992 Transport and Works Act, satisfy statutory safety regulations regarding machinery operation and substance limits.

However, most tests do not show that someone is under the influence or by how much. Without knowing any of these things, drug testing is often a poor measure of one's ability to perform.

The screening of recruits or routine testing of employees is argued on the basis that drug use reduces productivity or performance. Studies into the relationship between drug use and performance show that drug use on its own is not a strong predictor of poor performance. Only when drug use is problematic is there a likelihood that an individual's performance will suffer. Indeed, as the British Crime Survey shows, drug use is often an activity of those in successful employment (see Chapter 3).

Critics, therefore, often argue that testing is not a good indicator of dysfunctionality and performance, but is instead a way to identify deviance and investigate humans and their lifestyles. As such, it is an infringement on an individual's civil liberty by:

- requesting a sample for testing
- taking action following a positive test.

Objections have also been raised that drug testing is unfair to certain groups (eg, Afro-Caribbeans) who may be more likely to test positive for some drugs, such as cannabis, in some circumstances (see page 162).

Finally, testing does not come cheap, with costs up to £100 per employee for an alcohol and drugs test. If it is to be cost-effective, drug testing needs to be made part of a holistic drugs and alcohol policy that deals effectively with possible problem substance abuse.

11

Reading list

Chapter 1: Illicit drugs and their effects

Institute for the Study of Drug Dependence (1999) *Drug Abuse Briefing 7th edition*, London: ISDD.

Brands B et al (eds) (1998) *Drugs and Drug Abuse: A reference text*, 3rd edition, Toronto: Addiction Research Foundation.

Coomber R (1994) *Drugs and Drug Use in Society: A critical reader*, London: Greenwich University Press.

Glass I (ed) (1991) *The International Handbook of Addiction Behaviour*, London: Tavistock/Routledge.

Inaba D & Cohen W (1993) *Uppers, Downers, All Arounders: Physical and mental effects of psychoactive drugs*, 2nd edition, Ashland: CNS Production.

Lowinson J H et al (1997) *Substance Abuse: A comprehensive textbook*, 3rd edition, Baltimore: Williams and Wilkins.

Shulgin A & Shulgin A (1991) *Pihkal: A chemical love story*, Berkeley, Calif: Transform Press.

Shulgin A & Shulgin A (1997) *Pihkal: The continuation*, Berkeley, Calif: Transform Press.

Tyler A (1995) *Street Drugs*, 3rd edition, London: Hodder and Stoughton.

Chapter 2: Why people use drugs

Allen D (1999) 'Outside society: drugs and social exclusion', *DrugLink*, 14(4), pp 16-18.

Bell J (1996) 'Why do people use drugs?' in Wilkinson C & Saunders B *Perspectives on Addiction*, Perth: Montgomery, pp 40-46.

Goldberg T (1999) *Demystifying Drugs: A psychosocial perspective*, Basingstoke: Macmillan

Hesselbrock M N et al (1999) 'Theories of etiology of alcohol and other drug use disorders', in McCrady B S & Epstein E E *Addictions: A comprehensive guidebook* New York: Oxford University Press, pp 50-72.

McFadyean M (1997) *Drugswise: A practical guide for concerned parents about the use of illegal drugs*, Cambridge: Icon Books.

Oetting G & Cox V (1997) *Etiology and Prevention of Drug Use: The US National Institute of Drug Abuse research monographs*, 1991-1994, MD: NIDA.

Petraitis J, Flay B R & Miller T Q (1995) 'Reviewing theories of adolescent substance use: organizing pieces in the puzzle', *Psychological Bulletin*, 117(1), pp 67-86.

South N (1999) *Drugs: Cultures, controls and everyday life*, London: Sage

Stimson G V et al (ed) (1998) *Drug Use in London*, London: Centre for Research on Drugs and Health Behaviour.

Royal College of Psychiatrists (1987) *Drug Scenes: A report on drugs and drug dependence*, London: Royal College of Psychiatrists.

Wilson J (1998) 'Abuse and misuse: the ultimate hidden population', *DrugLink*, 13(4), pp 10-11.

Chapter 3: How many drug users are there?

Aldridge J, Parker H & Measham F (1999) *Drug Trying and Drug Use Across Adolescence: A longitudinal study of young people's drug taking in two regions of Northern England*, London: Home Office.

Balding J (1999) *Young people in 1998: and looking back as far as 1983: the health related behaviour questionnaire results for 18,221 young people aged 12-13 and 14-15 in 1998 and approximately 200,000 since 1983*, Exeter: Schools Health Education Unit.

Balding J (1998) *Young People and Illegal Drugs in 1998*, Exeter: Schools Health Education Unit.

Bradley A & Baker O (1999) 'Drugs in the United Kingdom: a jigsaw with missing pieces, in Office for National Statistics', *Social Trends 29*, London: The Stationery Office, pp 15-28.

Goddard E & Higgins V (1999) *Smoking, Drinking and Drug Use among Young Teenagers in 1998: Vol 1: England*, London: The Stationery Office, pp 106 and 109.

Institute for the Study of Drug Dependence (1999) *UK Drug Situation 1999: A report by ISDD* London: ISDD.

MacDonald Z (1999) 'Illicit drug use in the UK: evidence from the British Crime Survey', *British Journal of Criminology*, 39(4), pp 585-608.

Ramsay, M & Partridge S (1999) *Drug Misuse Declared in 1998: Results from the British crime survey*, Home Office Research Study 197, London: Home Office.

Chapter 4: How do drugs affect children and the family?

Briggs G, Freeman R K & Yaffe S J (1998) *Drugs in Pregnancy and Lactation: A reference guide to fetal and neonatal risk*, 5th edition Baltimore, Maryland: Williams & Wilkins.

Department of Health (1999) *Working Together to Safeguard Children: A guide to inter-agency working to safeguard and promote the welfare of children: consultation draft*, London: DoH.

Dorn N, Ribbens J & South N (1994) *Coping with a Nightmare: Family feelings about long-term drug use*, London: ISDD.

Finnegan L P, 'Addiction and pregnancy: maternal and child issues', in Tagliamonte A & Maremmani I *Drug addiction and related clinical problems* Vienna: Springer, 1995, pp 137-47.

Kaufman E & Kaufman P (1992) *Family Therapy of Drug and Alcohol Abuse*, 2nd edition, London: Allyn and Bacon.

Kendler K S, Davis C G, & Kessler R C (1997) 'The familiar aggregation of common psychiatric and substance use disorders in the national comorbidity survey: a family history study', *British Journal of Psychiatry*, 1997, 170, pp 541-48.

Klee H & Jackson M (1998) *Illicit Drug Use, Pregnancy and Early Motherhood*, Manchester: SRHSA, Manchester Metropolitan University.

McFadyean M (1997) *Drugs Wise: A practical guide for concerned parents about the use of illegal drugs*, Cambridge: Icon Books.

Mounteney J (1999) *Drugs, Pregnancy and Childcare: A guide for professionals*, revised edition, London: ISDD.

Siney C (ed) (1995) *The Pregnant Drug Addict*, Hale, Cheshire: Books for Midwives Press.

Velleman R et al (1993) 'The families of problem drug users: a study of 50 close relatives', *Addiction*, 88(9), pp 1281-89.

Chapters 5a & 5b: Drugs and crime

Bennett T & UK Home Office (1998) *Drugs and Crime: The results of research on drug testing and interviewing arrestees*, London: HMSO.

Bucknell P & Ghodse H (1997) *Misuse of Drugs*, 3rd edition, London: Sweet and Maxwell.

Department of Health (1999) *NTORS: Two year outcomes: the National Treatment Outcome Study: changes in substance use, health and crime*, London: DoH.

Healey A et al (1998) 'Economic burden of drug dependence: social costs incurred by drug users at intake to the National Treatment Outcome Research Study', *British Journal of Psychiatry*, 173, pp 160-65.

Hough M (1996) *Drugs Misuse and the Criminal Justice System: a review of the literature*, London: Home Office, DPI Paper 15.

McBride D C & McCoy C B (1997) 'The drugs-crime relationship: an analytical framework', in McShane M and Williams F P (eds) *Drug Use and Drug Policy*, New York: Garland, pp 223-44.

Rothbard A et al (1999) 'Revisiting the effectiveness of methadone treatment on crime reductions in the 1990s', *Journal of Substance Abuse Treatment*, 16(4), pp 329-35.

Chapter 6: What are the arguments for and against legalising prohibited drugs?

Inciardi J A (ed) (1991) *The Drug Legalization Debate*, Newbury Park, NY: Sage, Studies in crime, law and justice volume 7.

Murji K (1995) 'The drug legalisation debate', *Sociology Review*, 4(3), pp 14-17.

Newcombe R (1999) 'The people on drugs: British attitudes to drugs laws and policy', *DrugLink*, 14(4), pp 12-15.

Ruggiero V (1999) 'Drugs as a password and the law as a drug: discussing the legalisation of illicit substances', in South N (ed) *Drugs: Cultures, controls and everyday life* London: Sage, p123-37.

Schaler J A (ed) (1998) *Drugs: Should we legalize, decriminalize or deregulate?* New York: Prometheus.

Chapter 7: What are the UK's anti-drug strategies?

Advisory Council for the Misuse of Drugs (1998) *Drug misuse and the environment: a report*, London: HMSO.

Coomber R (ed) (1998) *The control of drugs and drug users: reason or reaction?*, Amsterdam: Harwood Academic Publishers.

HM Government (1995) *Tackling Drugs Together: A strategy for England 1995-1998*,

London: HMSO
Institute for the Study of Drug Dependence (1999) *UK Drug Situation: 1999*,
London: ISDD
Stimson G, Des Jarlais D C & Ball A L (eds) (1998) *Drug injecting and HIV infection: global dimensions and local responses*, London: University College London.

Chapter 8: Where to get help
Brady K T, Halligan P & Malcolm R J (1999) 'Dual diagnosis', in Galanter M &
Kleber H D (eds) *Textbook of Substance Abuse Treatment*, Washington, DC:
American Psychiatric Press, pp 475-83.
Ghodse H (1995) *Drugs and Addictive Behaviour: A guide to treatment*, 2nd edition, Oxford: Blackwell Science.
Gossop M et al (1999) 'Methadone treatment practices and outcome for opiate
addicts treated in drug clinics and in general practice: results from the National
Treatment Outcome Research Study', *British Journal of General Practice*: 1999, 49
(438), pp 31-34.
Gossop M & Marsden J (1996) 'Assessment and treatment of opiate problems', in
Rommelspacher H (ed) *Drugs of Abuse* London: Bailliere Tindall, 1996 pp 445-59.
Gossop M et al (1999) 'Treatment evaluation in the UK: the National Treatment
Outcome Research Study', in Baker O & Mounteney J (eds) *Evaluating the treatment of drug abuse in the European Union*, Luxembourg: Office for Official
Publications of the European Communities, pp 67-74.
Lowinson J H et al (eds) (1997) *Substance Abuse: A comprehensive textbook*, 3rd
edition, Baltimore, Md: Williams and Wilkins, xxvi, 956p.
Marsden J (1998) 'Opiate substitution: critical issues and future directions', *Journal
of Drug Issues*, 28(1), pp 243-63.
Marsden J (1998) 'Cocaine in Britain: prevalence, problems and treatment
responses', *Journal of Drug Issues*: 1998, 28(1), pp 225-41.
Robertson R (ed) (1998) *Management of Drug Users in the Community: A practical
handbook*, London: Arnold.

Chapter 9: Drugs and the media
Cohen J (1996) 'Drug education: politics, propaganda and censorship',
International Journal of Drug Policy, 7(3), pp 153-157.
Hastings G & Stead M (1999) *Using the Media in Drugs Prevention*, London: Drugs
Prevention Initiative.
Murji K (1998) 'The agony and the ecstasy: drugs, media and morality', in
Coomber R *The Control of Drugs and Drug Users: Reason or reaction?*, Amsterdam:
Harwood Academic Publishers, pp 69-85.

Chapter 10: Drug myths
Coomber R (1997) 'The adulteration of illicit drugs with dangerous substances:
the discovery of a "myth"', *Contemporary Drug Problems*, 24(2).
Davies J B (1997) *The Myth of Addiction*, 2nd edition, Harwood.

Ditton J & Hammersley R (1994) 'The typical cocaine user: how our blinkered vision of the cocaine users has created the myth of cocaine irresistibility', *DrugLink*, 9(6), pp 11-14.

Gabe J (ed) (1991) *Understanding Tranquilliser Use: The role of the social sciences*, Routledge.

Goldberg T (1999) *Demystifying Drugs: A psychosocial perspective*, Basingstoke: Macmillan.

Gossop M (1996) *Living with Drugs*, 4th edition, Aldershot: Arena.

Tyler A (1995) *Street Drugs*, 3rd edition, London: Hodder & Stoughton.

Chapter 11: What is drug testing?

Bowers L D (1998) 'Athletic drug testing', *Cline Sport MEd*, 1998, 17 (2), pp 299-318.

Jackson T (1999) *Drugs and Alcohol Policies*, London: Institute of Personnel and Development.

McKibben M A & Fielding L (1999) *Drink, Drugs and Work Don't Mix: Promoting drug and alcohol policies in the workplace*, London: ISDD.

Meadway C, Parmar S &George S (1999) 'Positively negative: drug testing uncovered', *DrugLink*, 1999, 14(6), pp 11-13.

Index